MW01461911

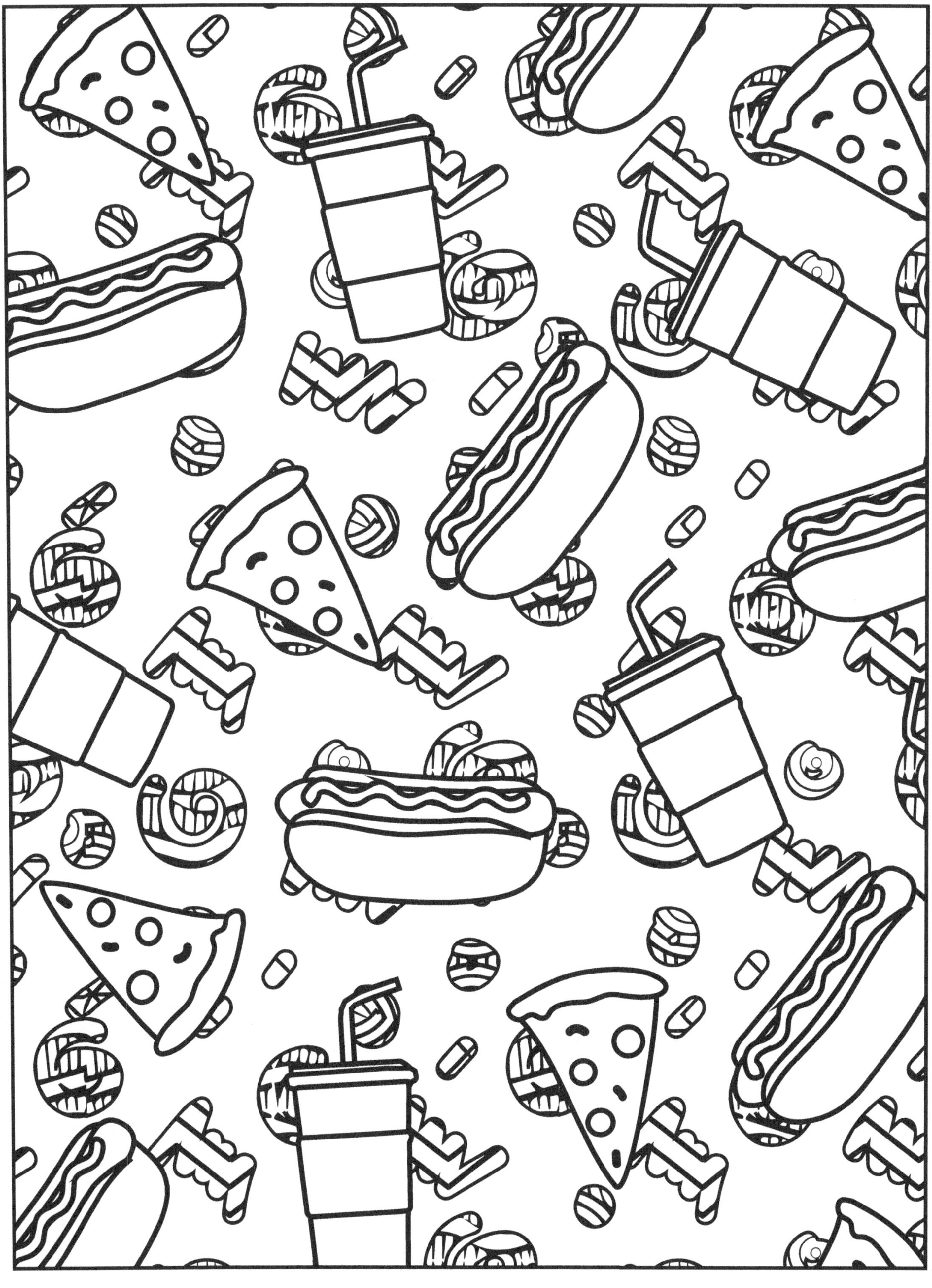

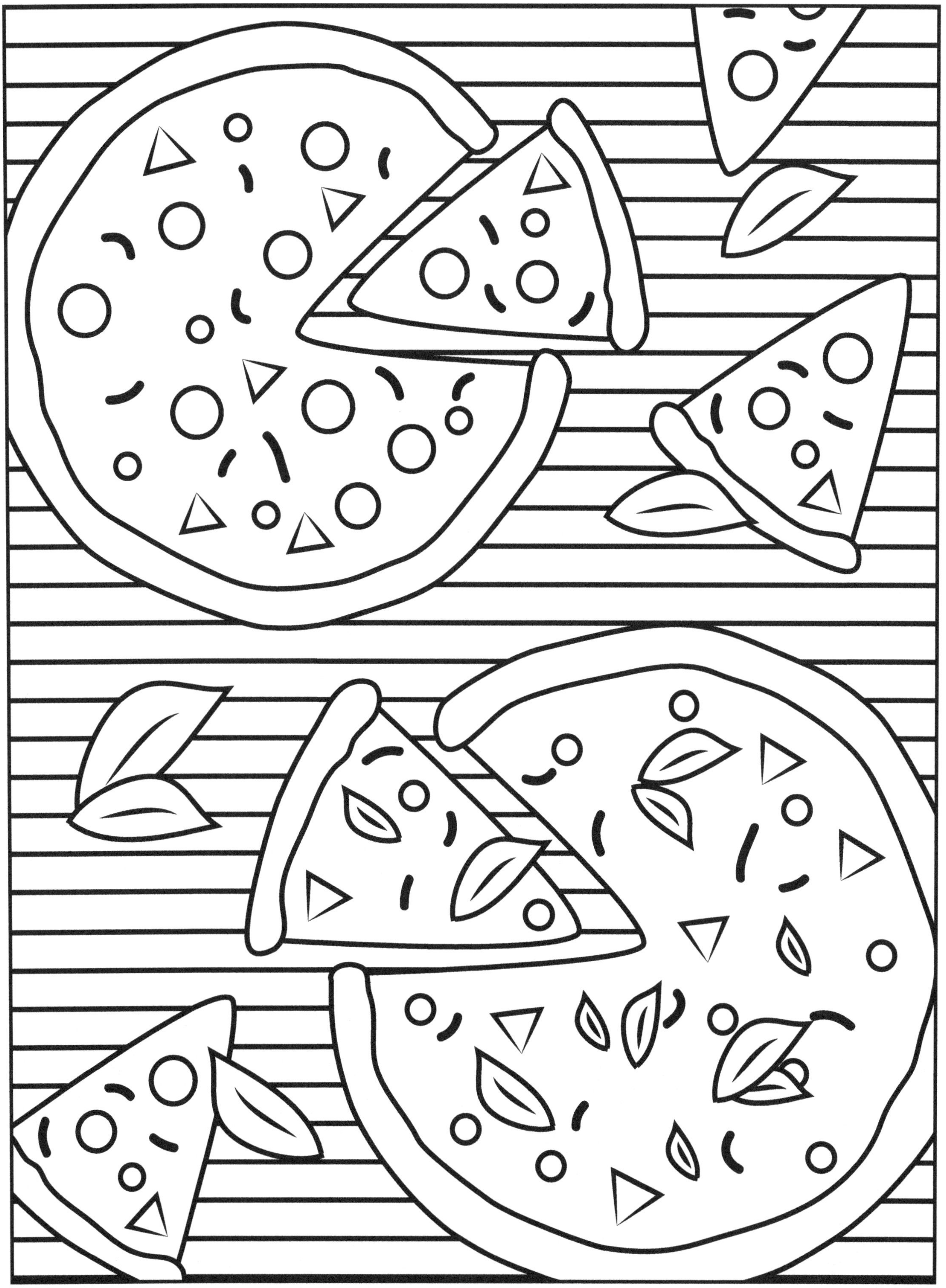

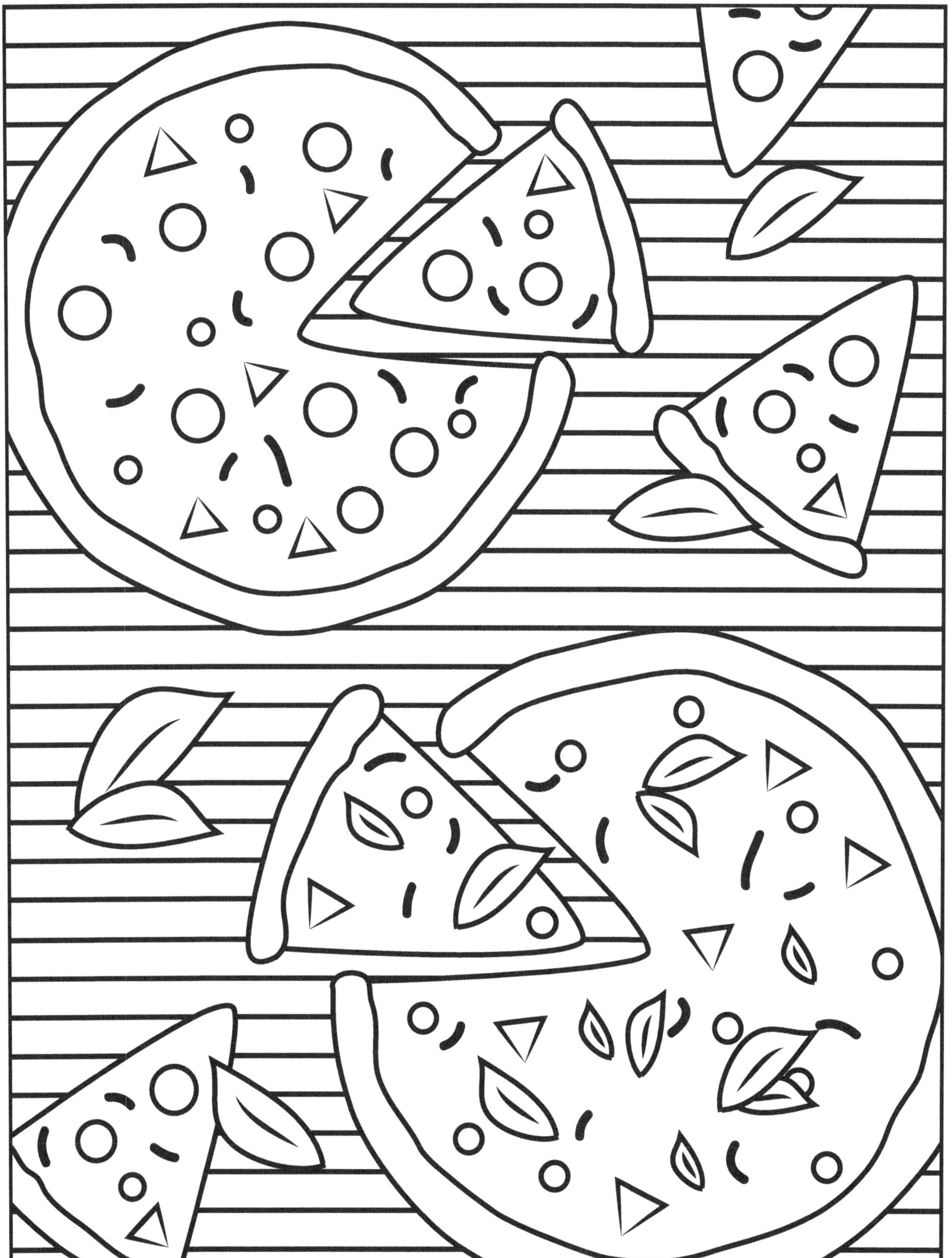

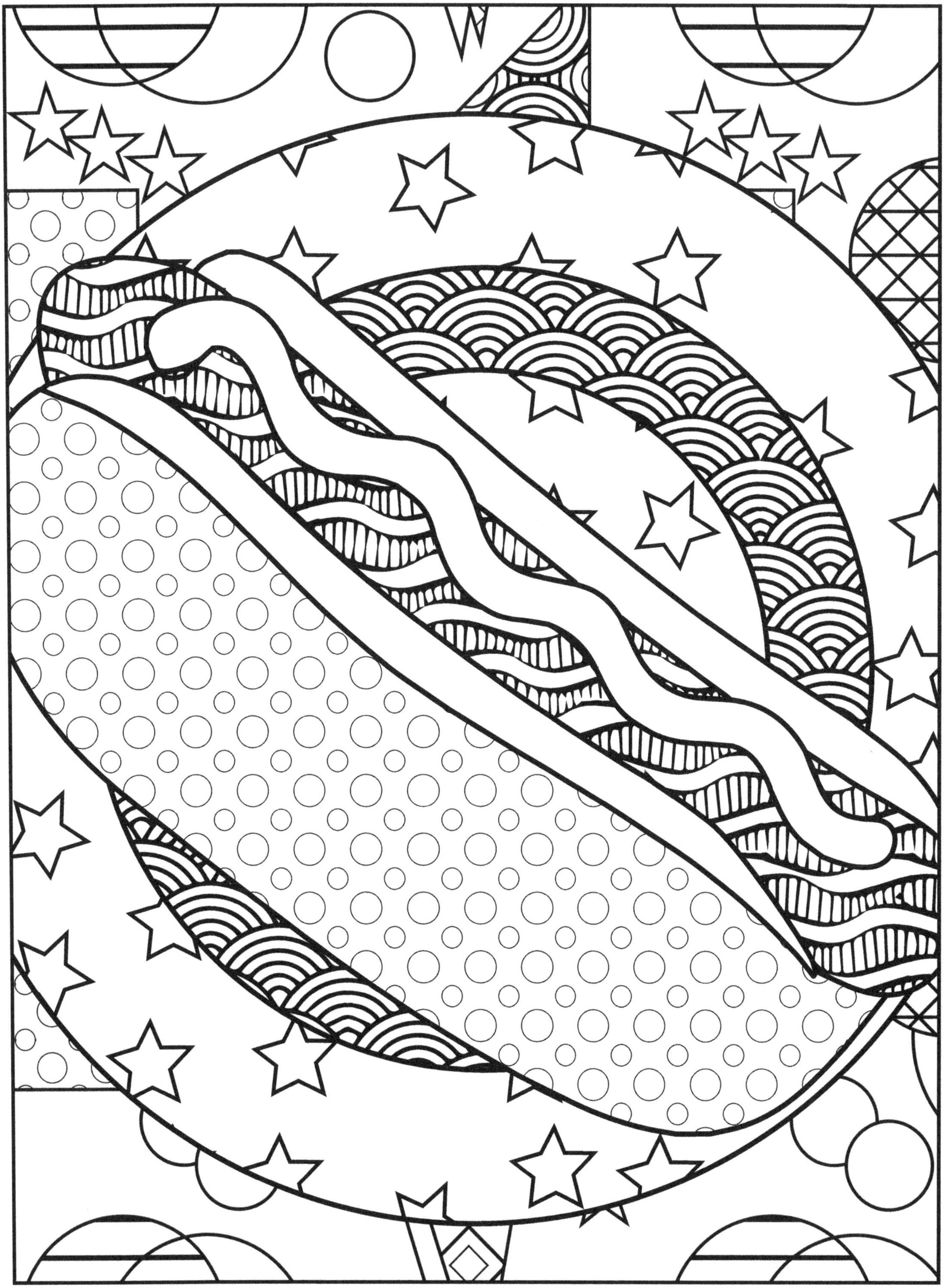

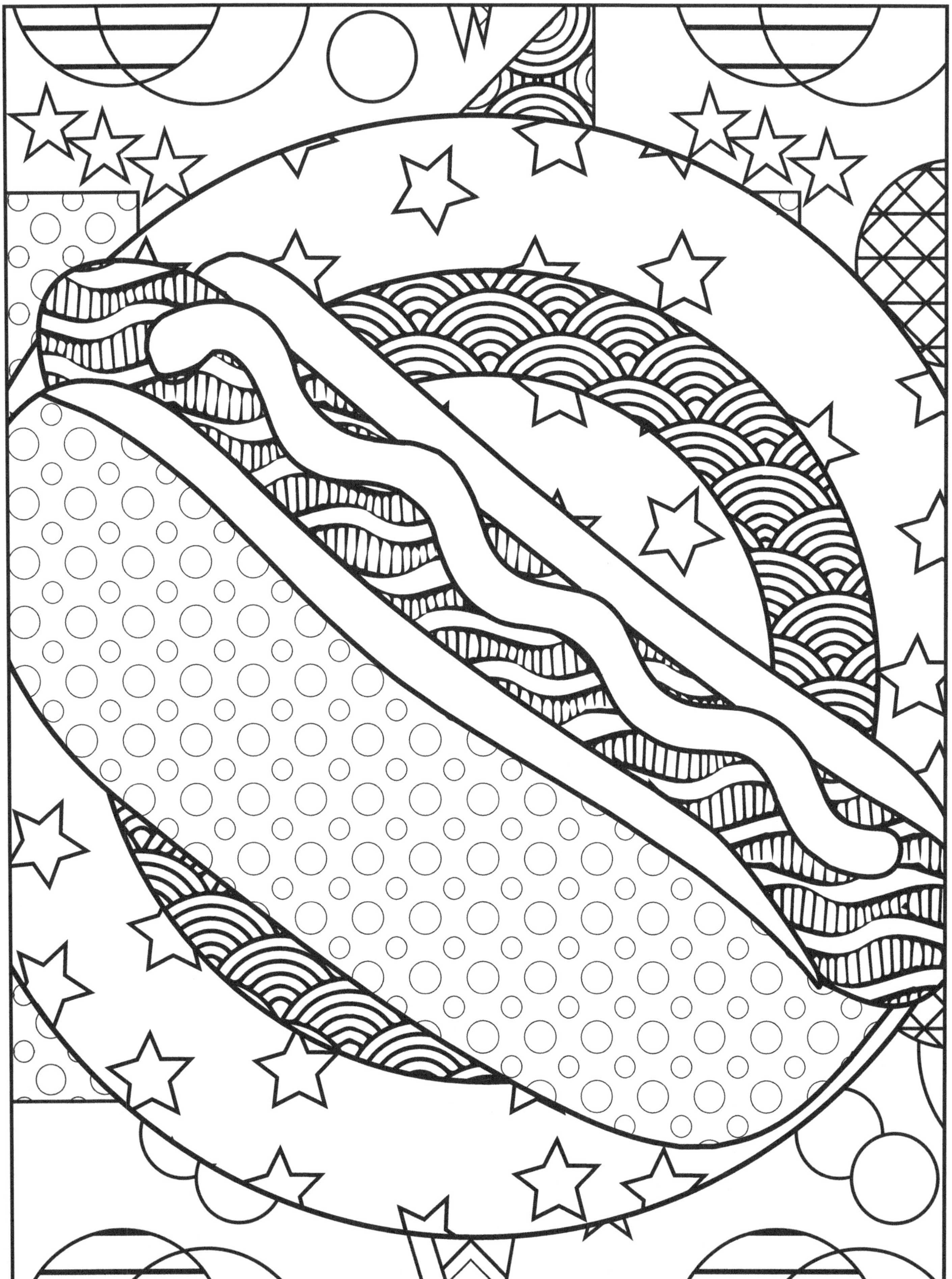

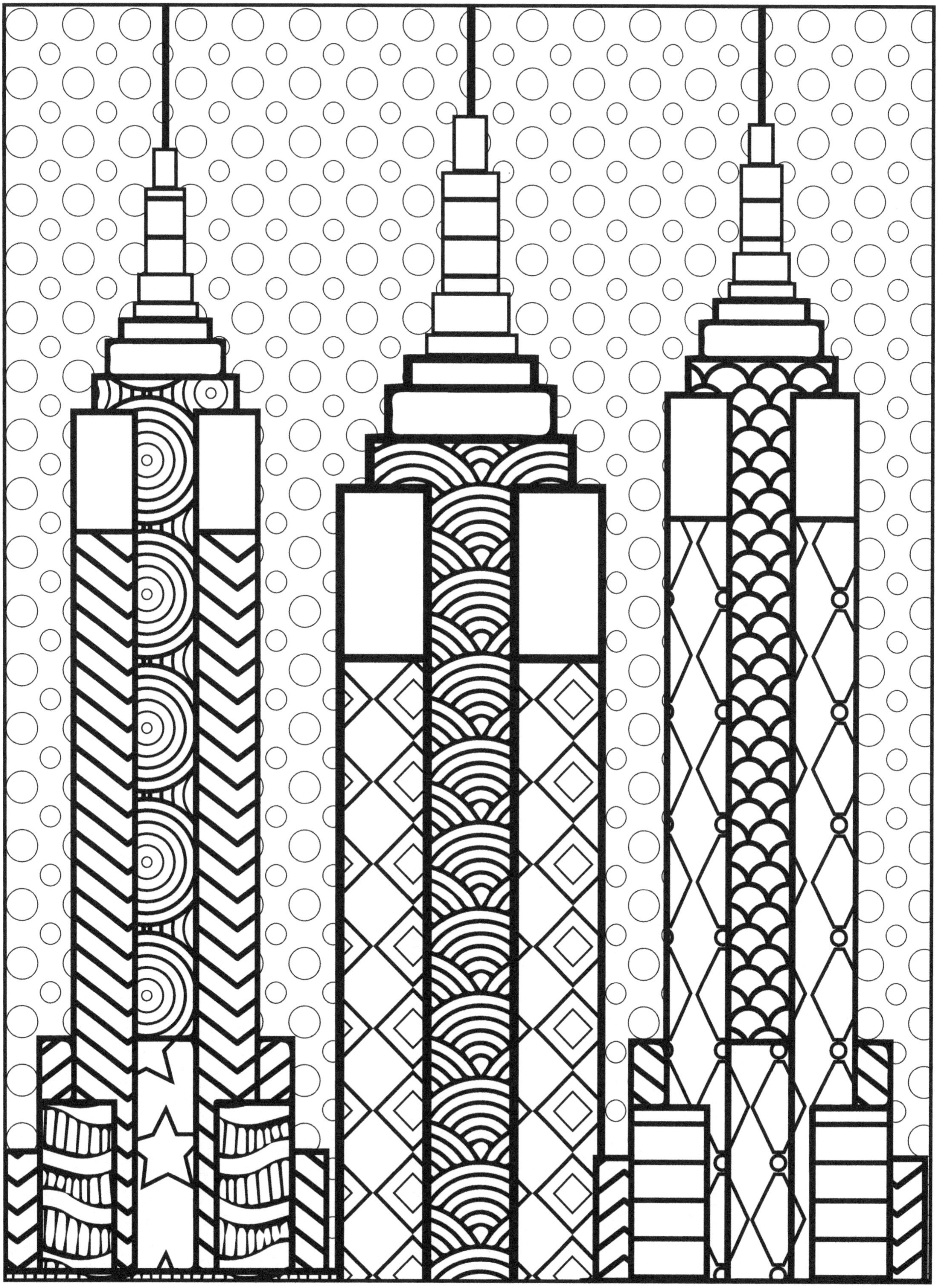

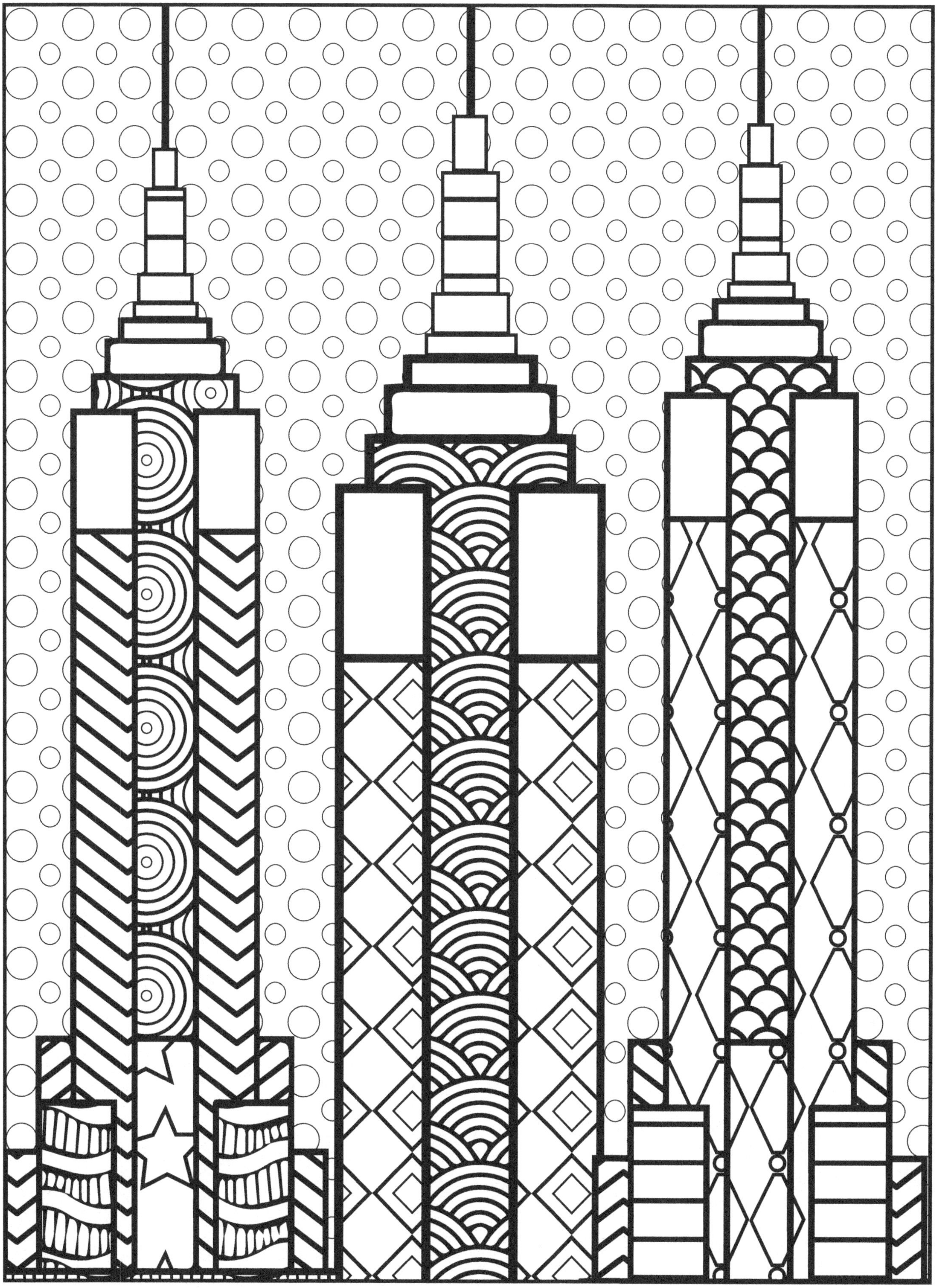

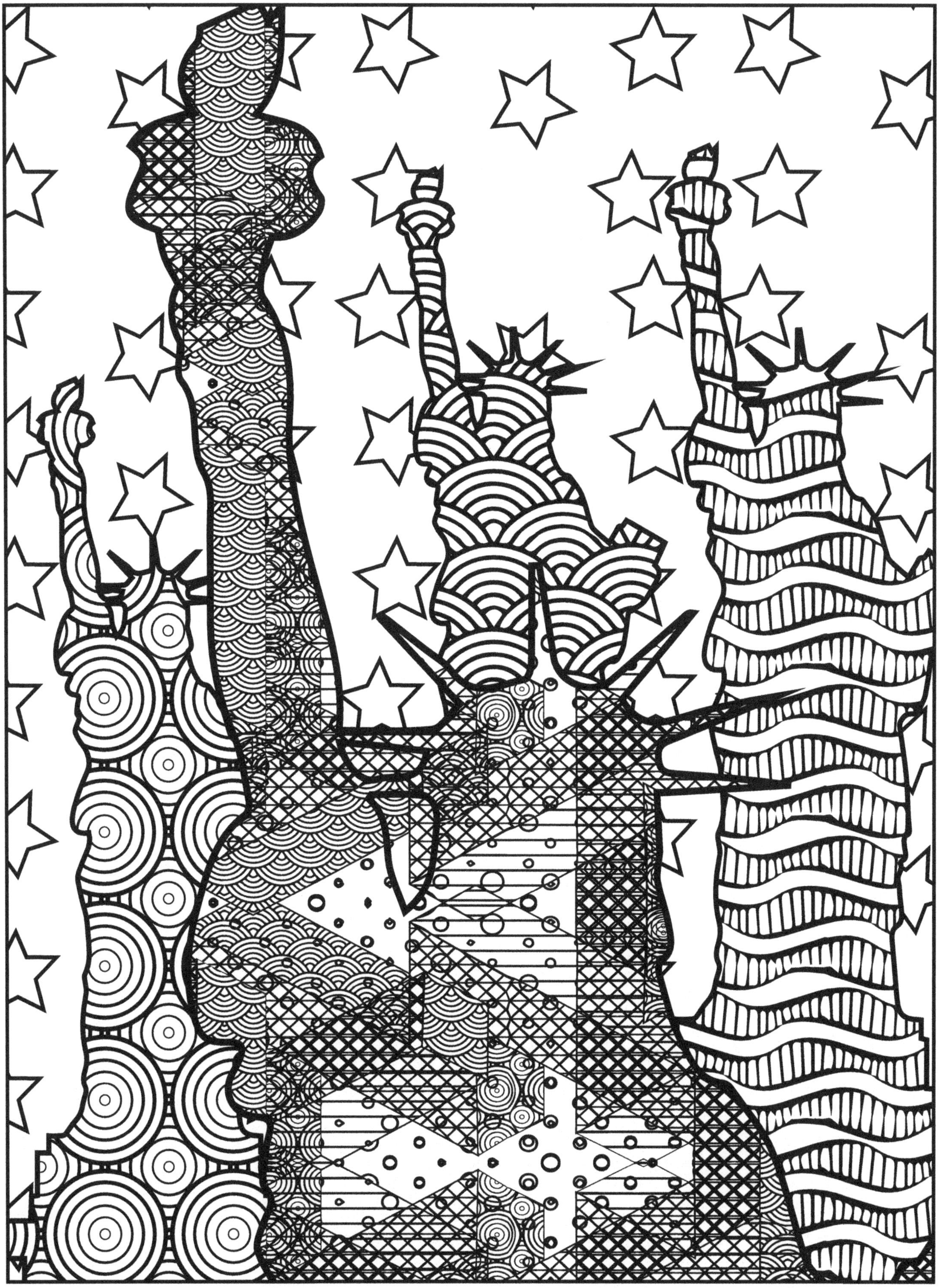

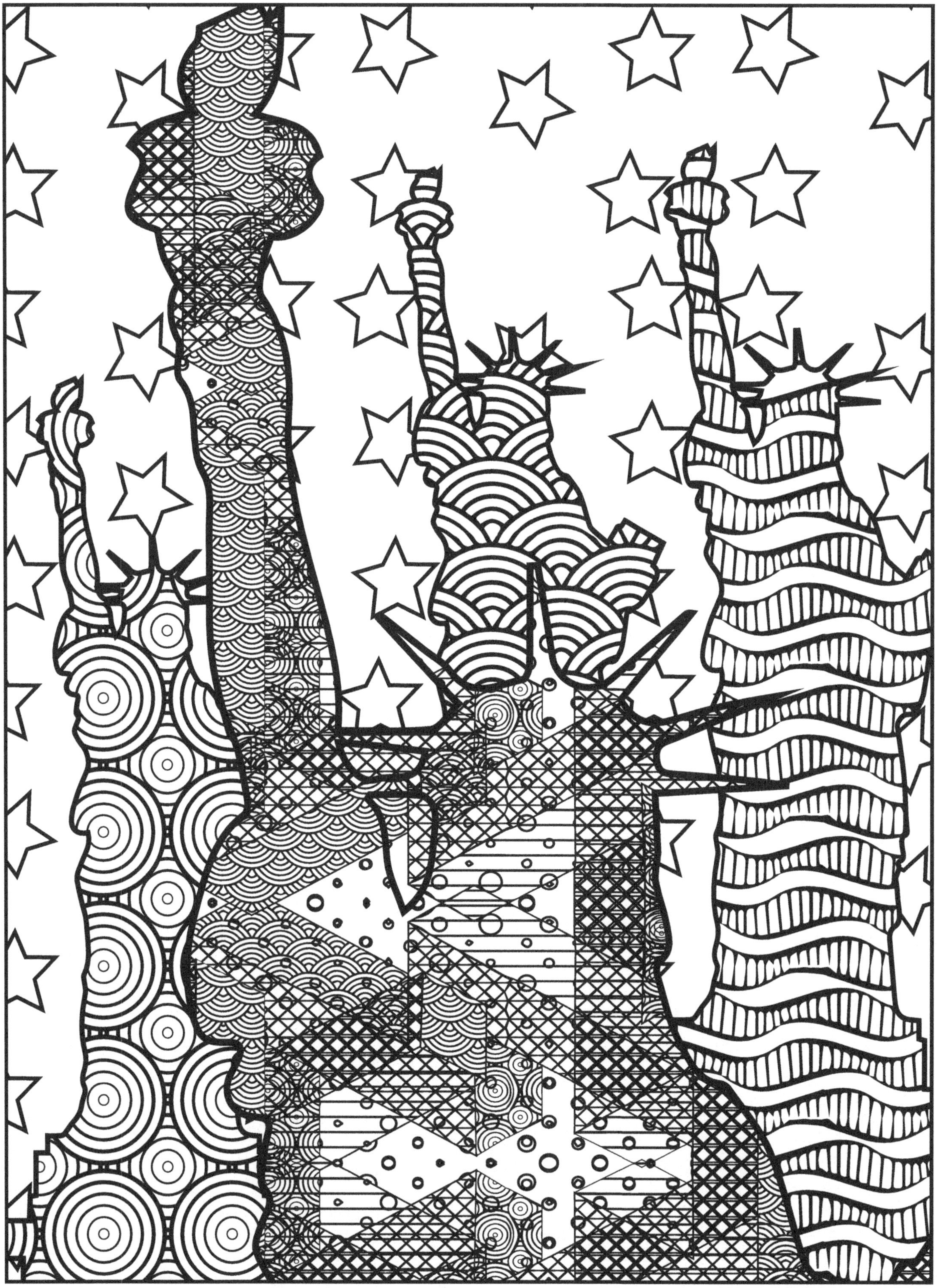

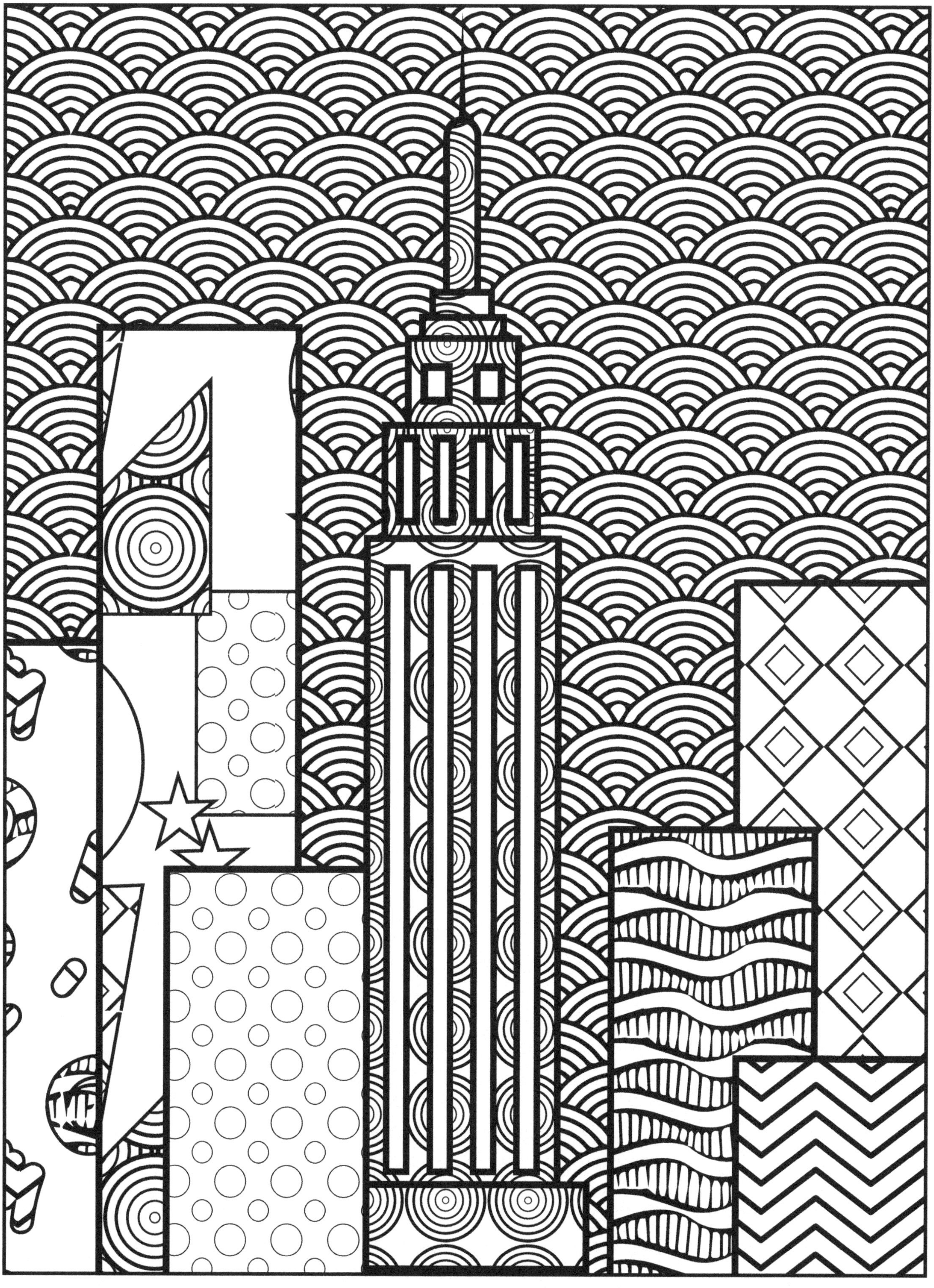

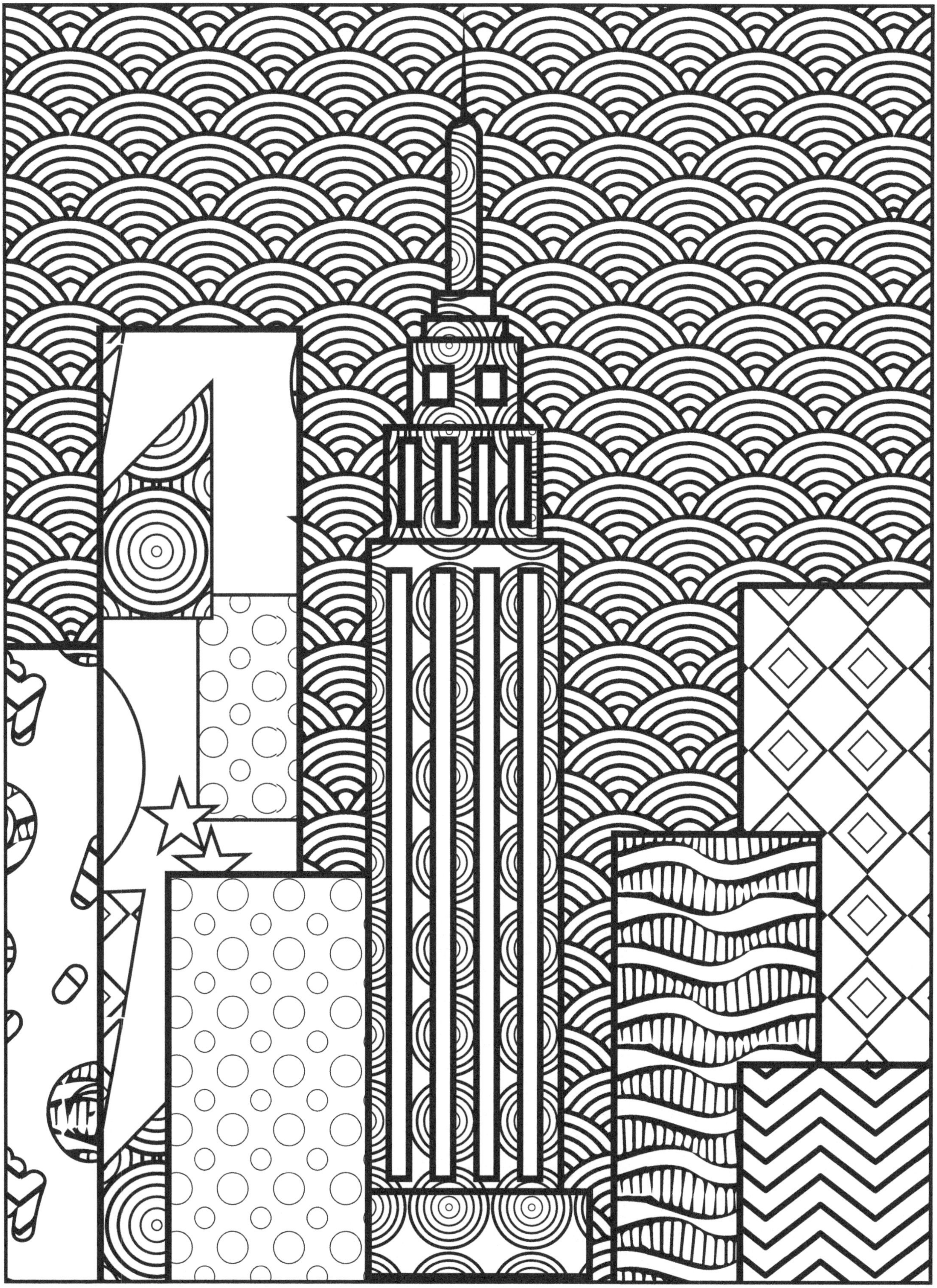

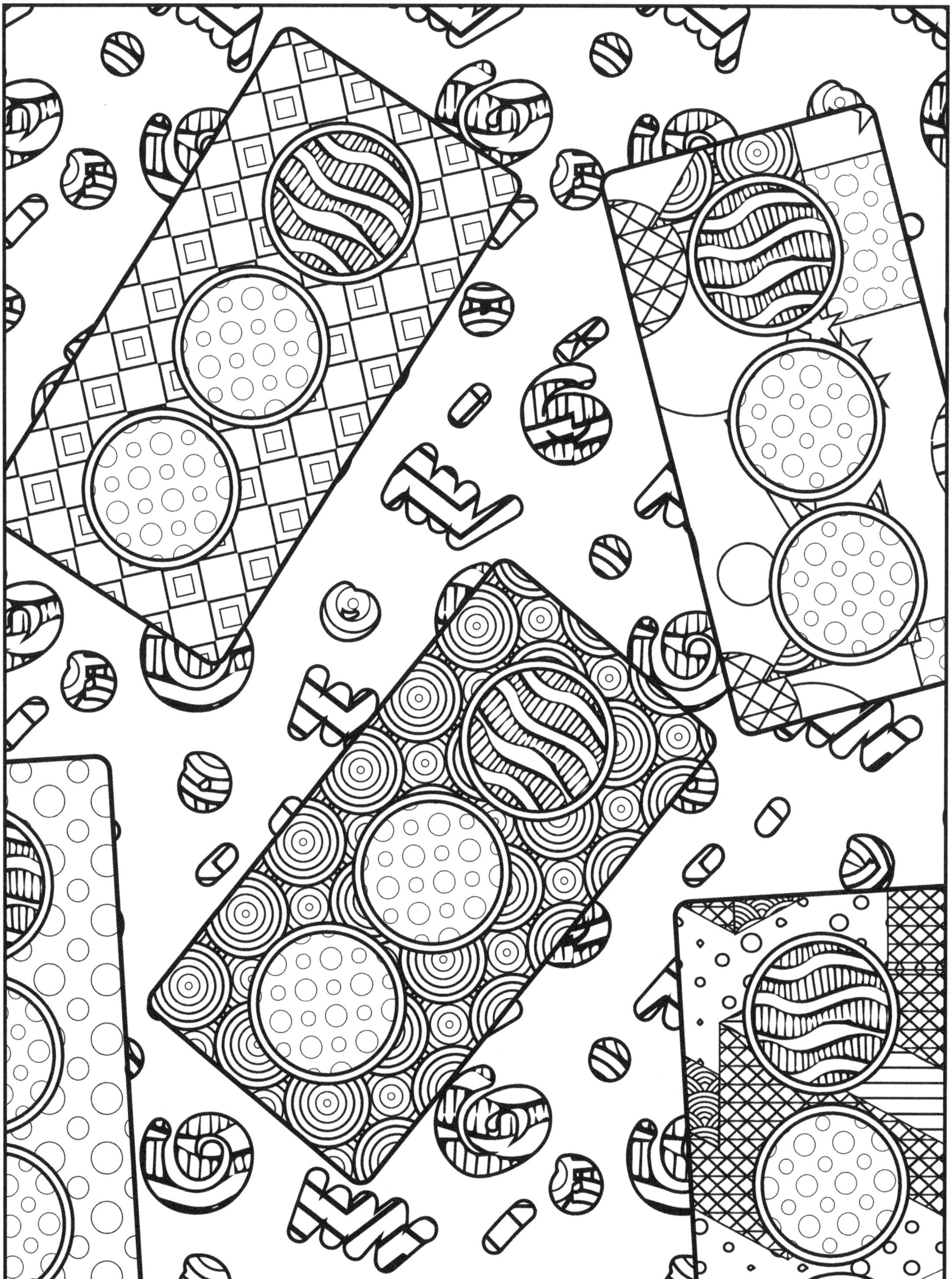

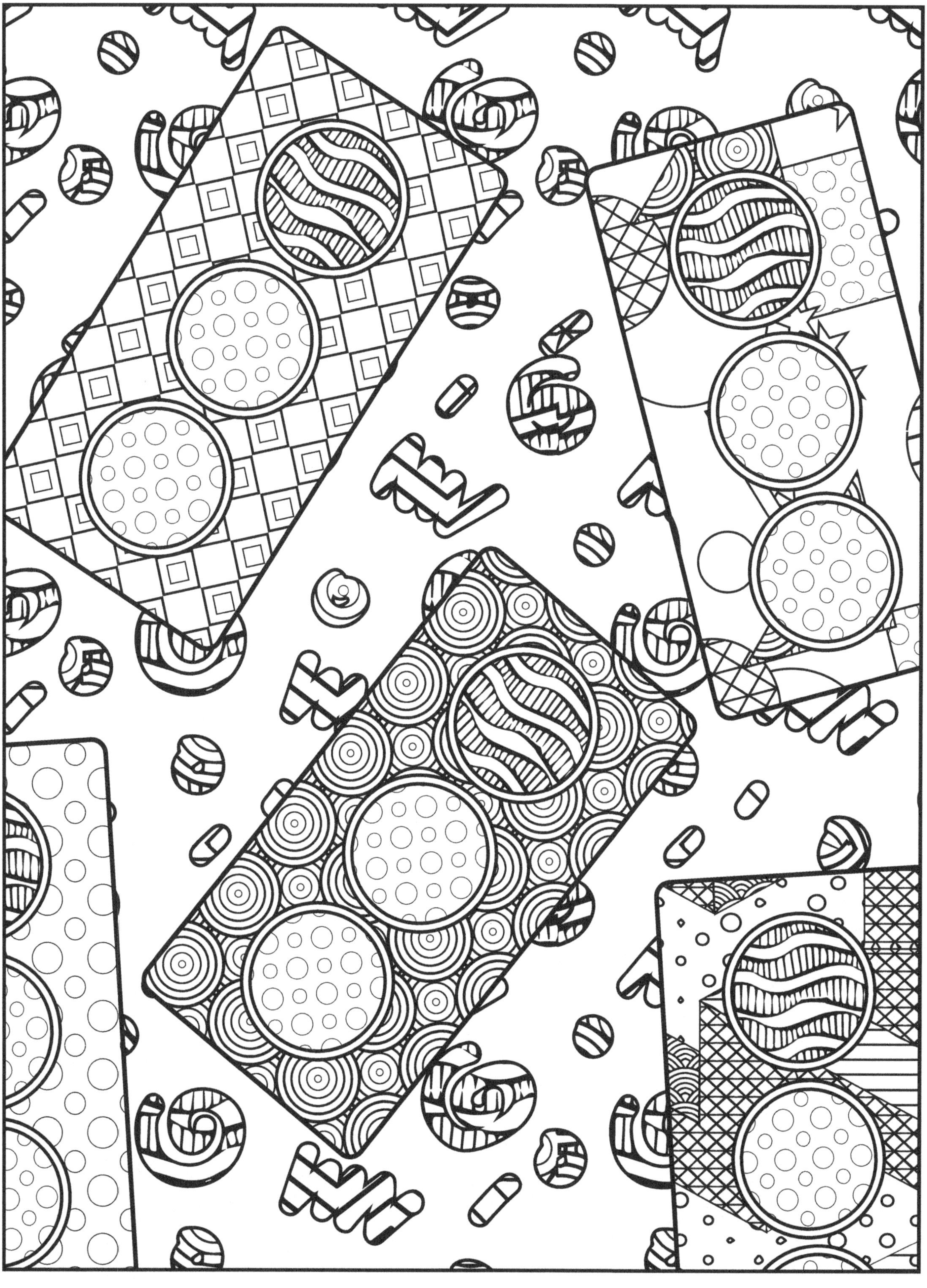

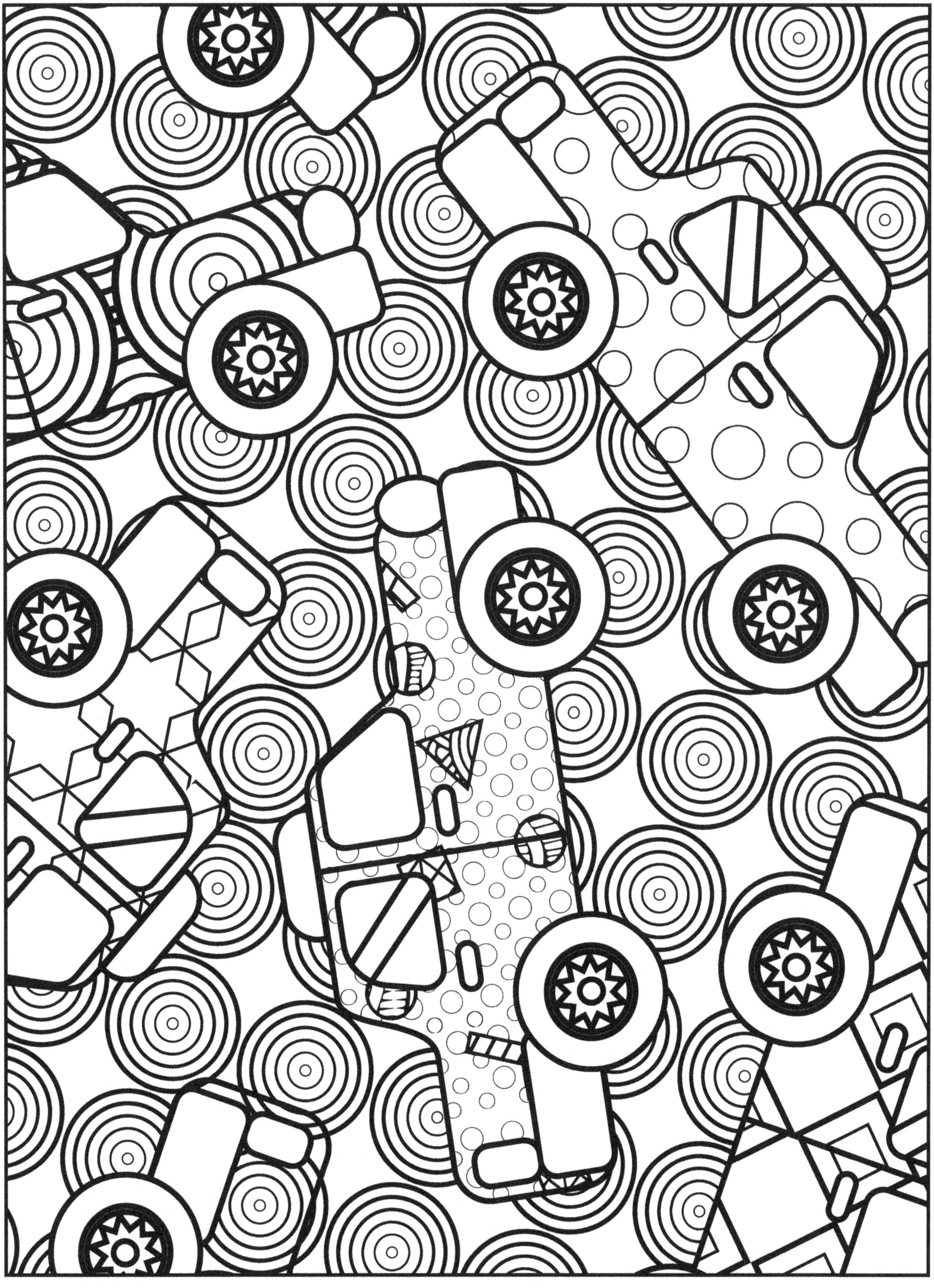

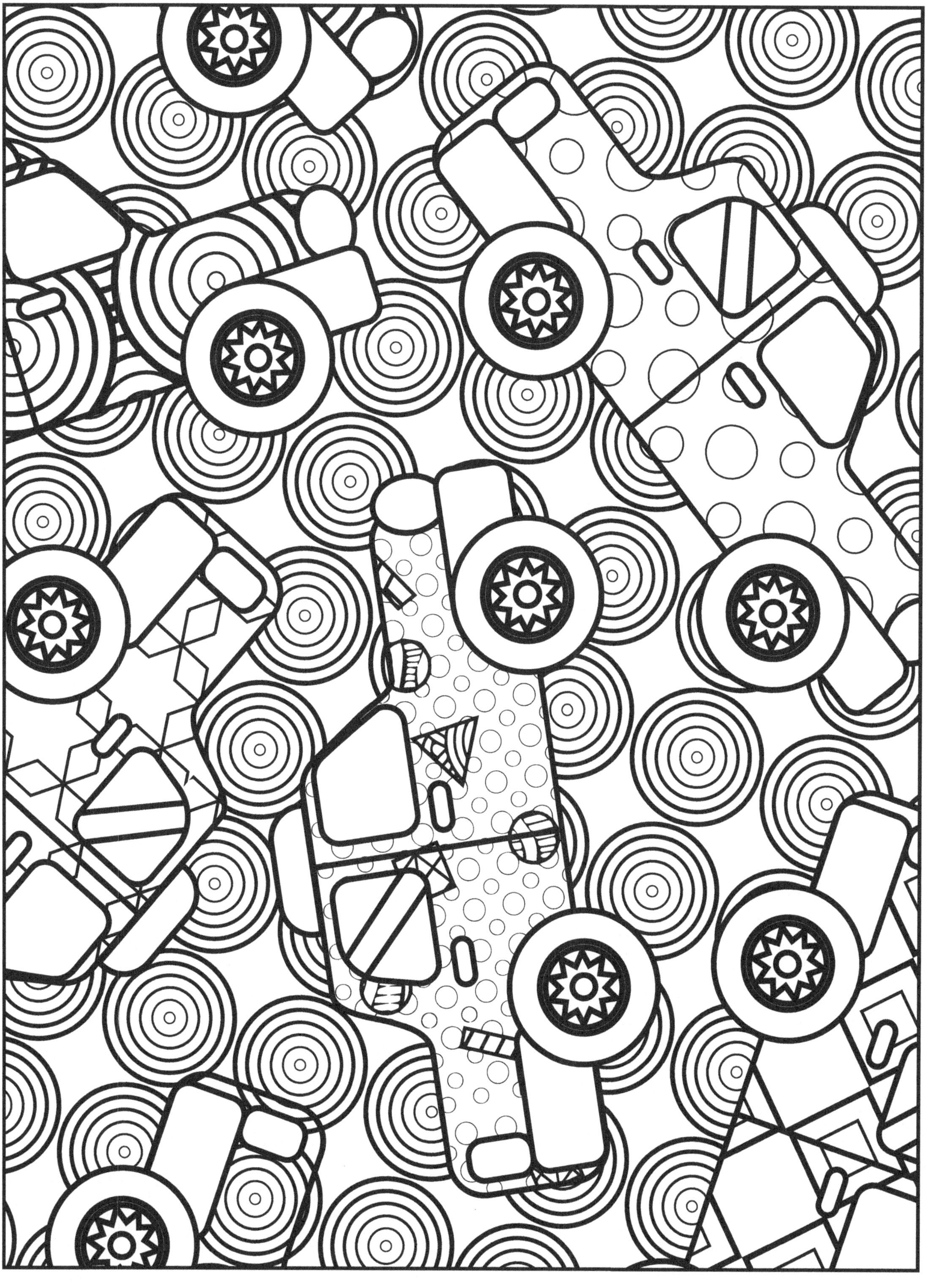

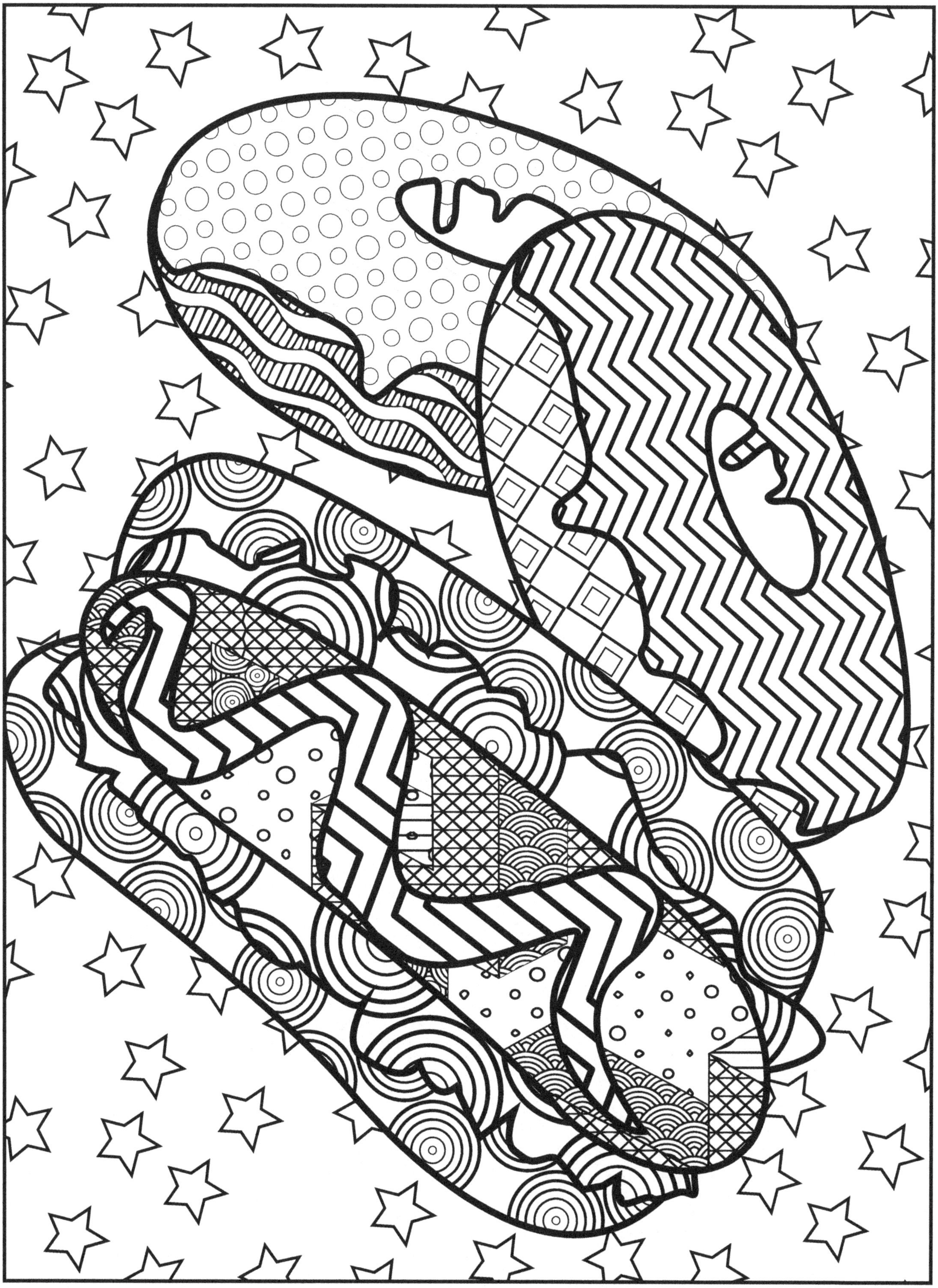

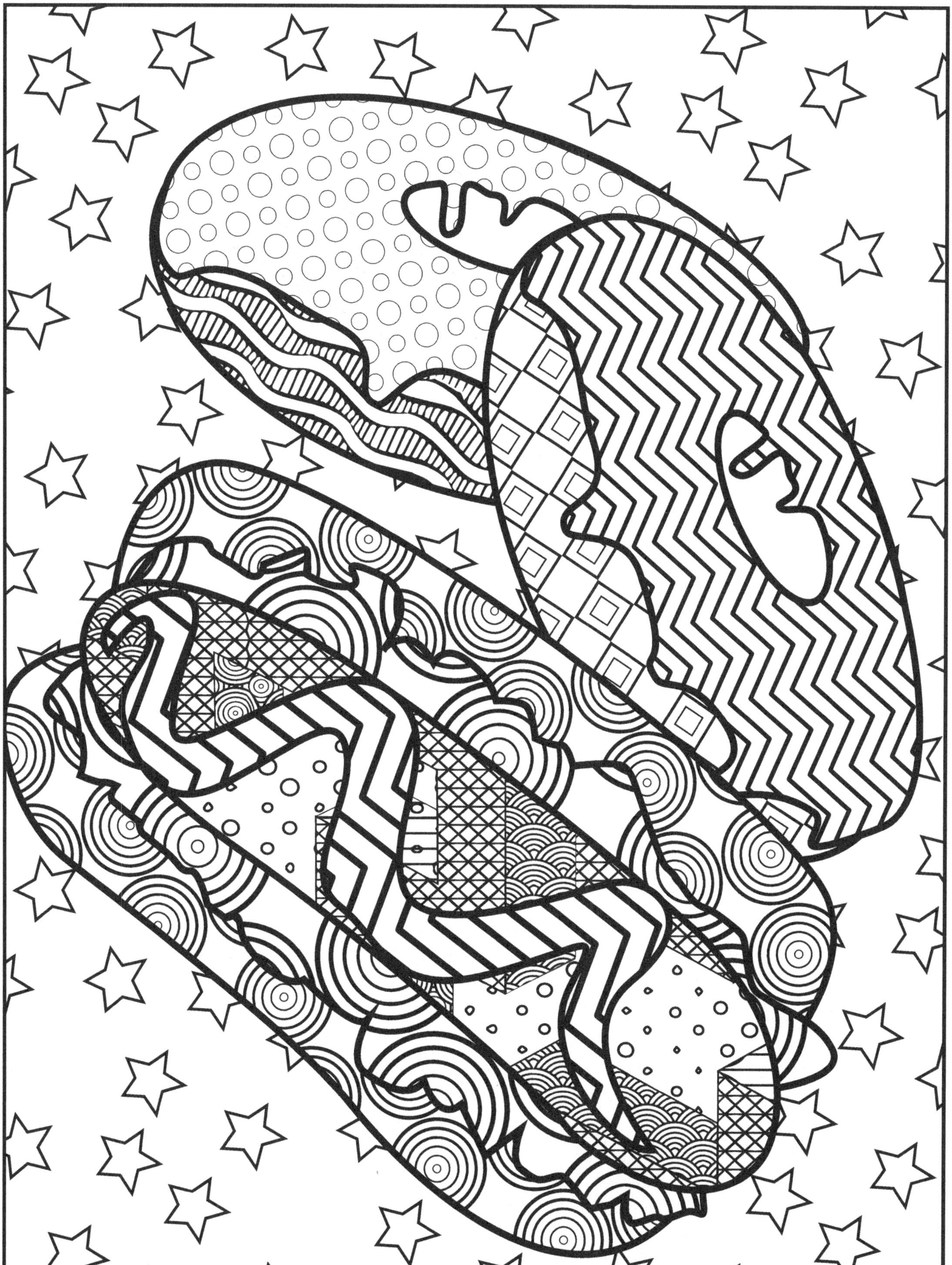

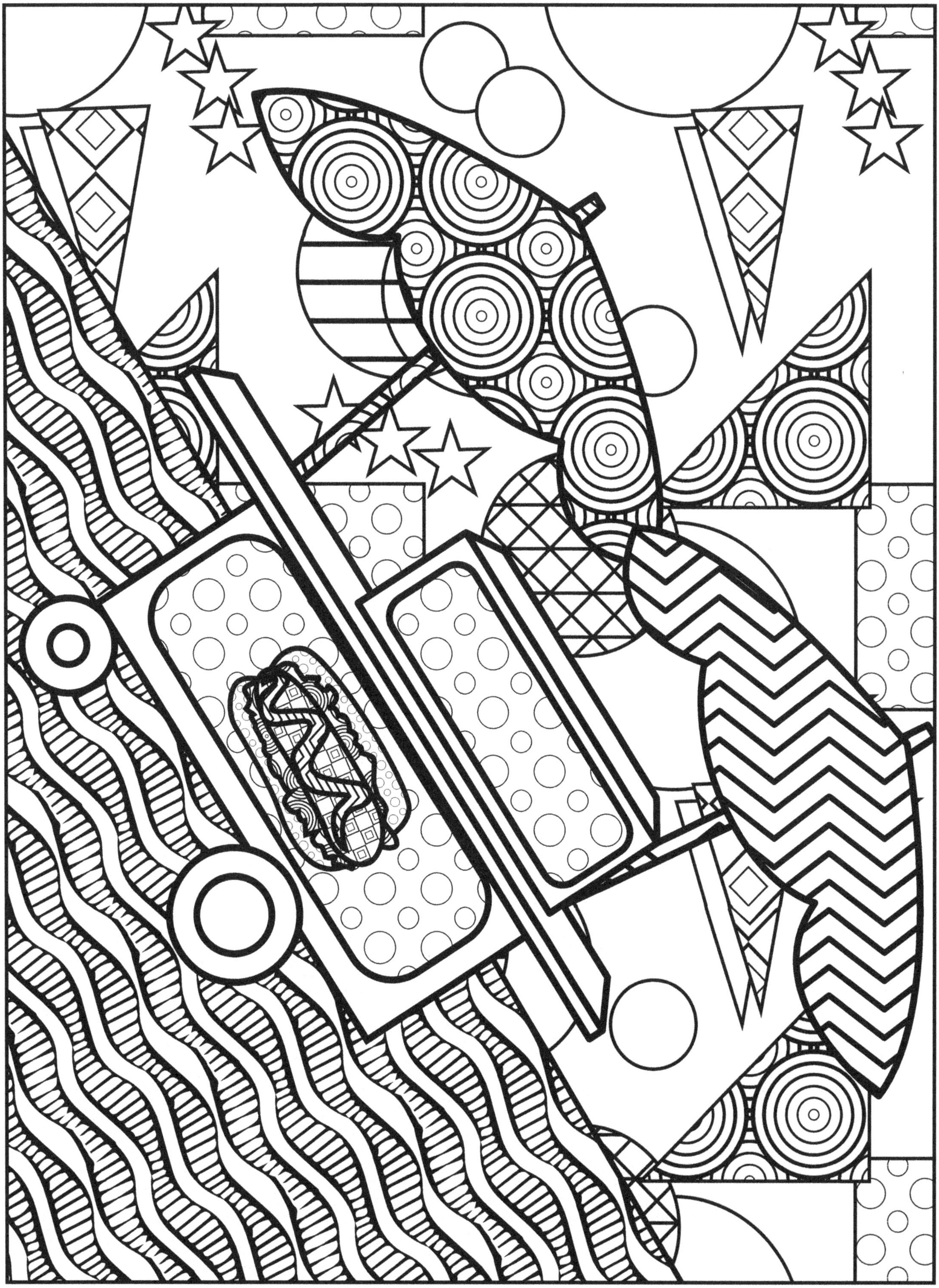

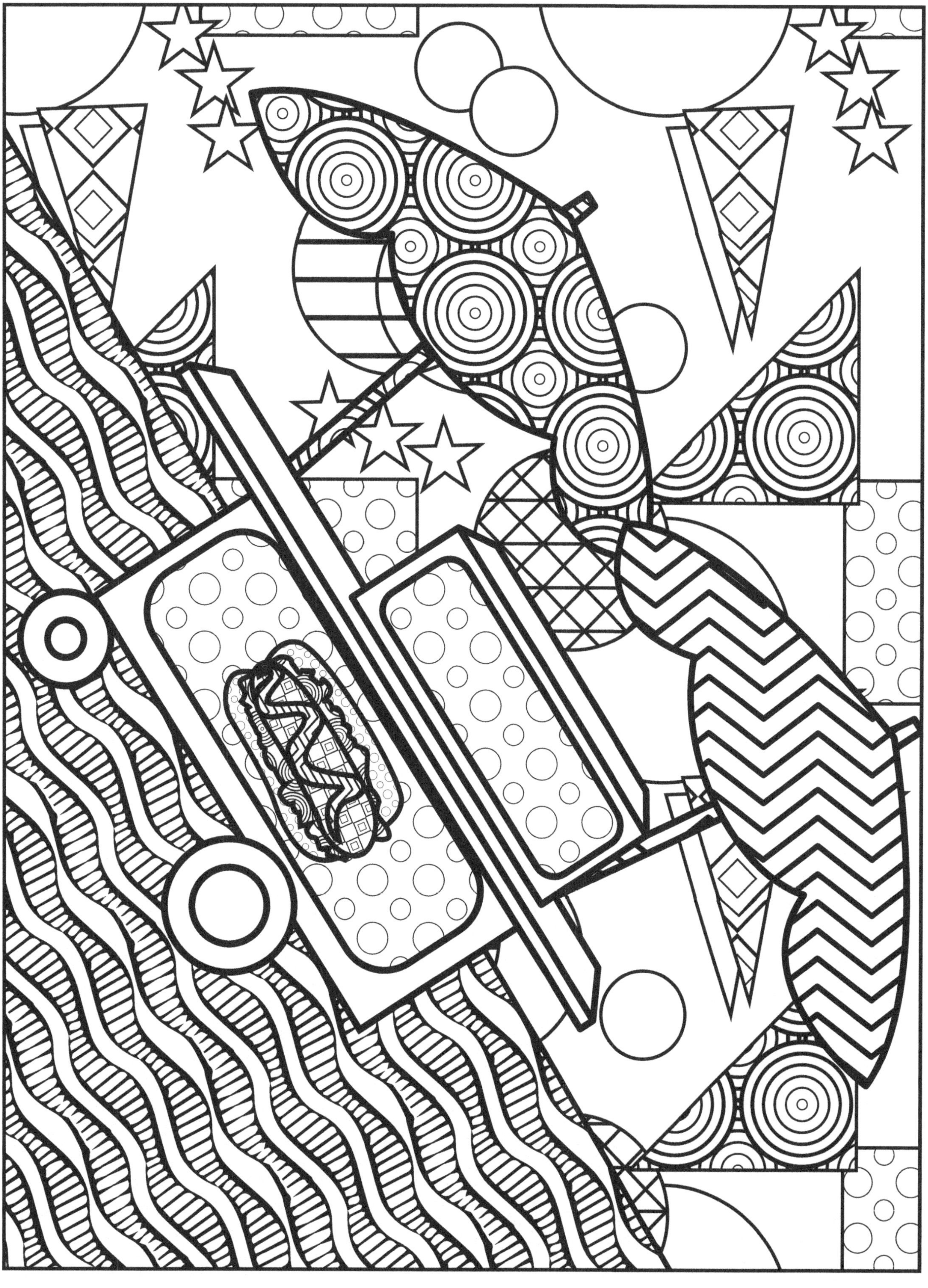

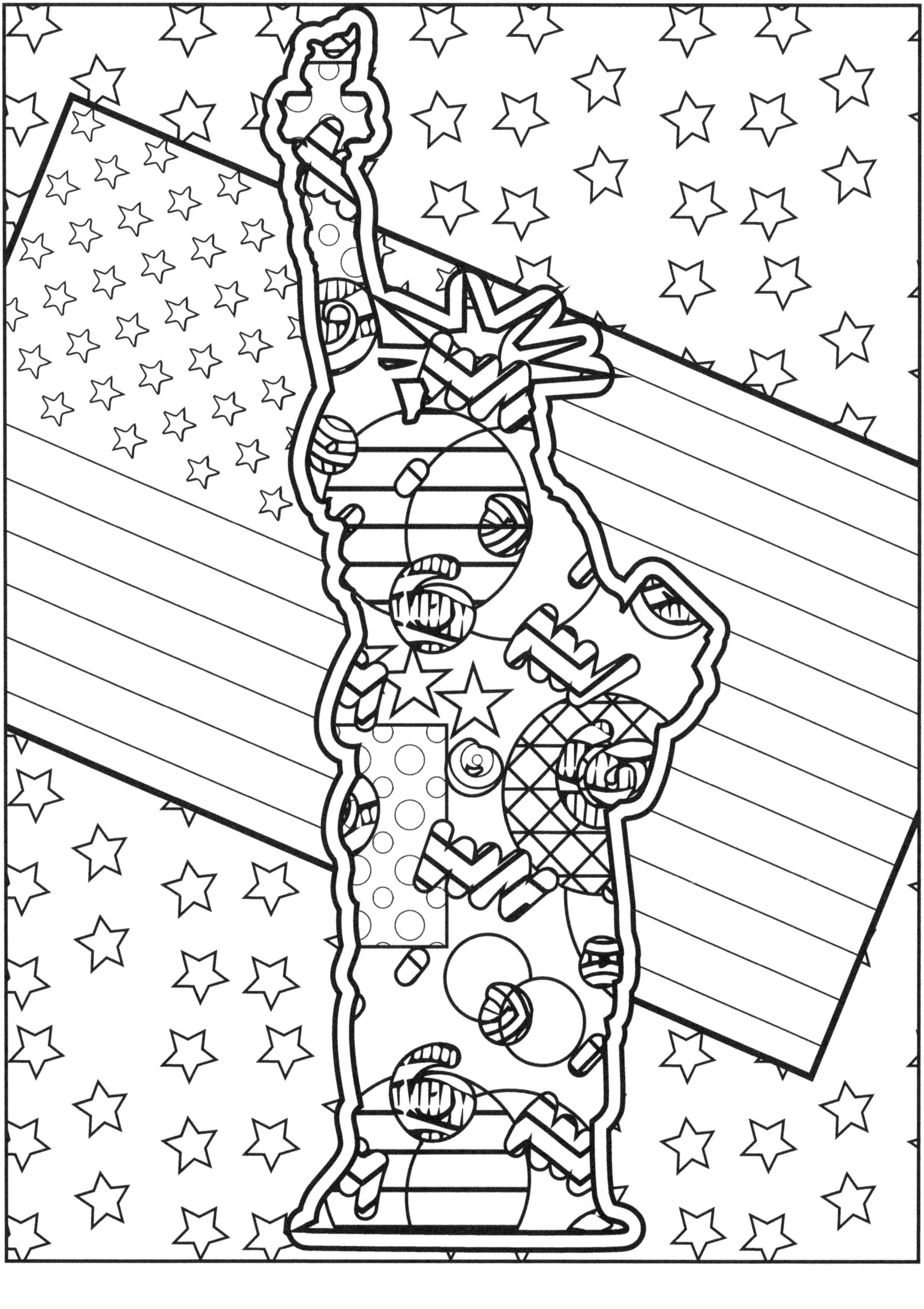

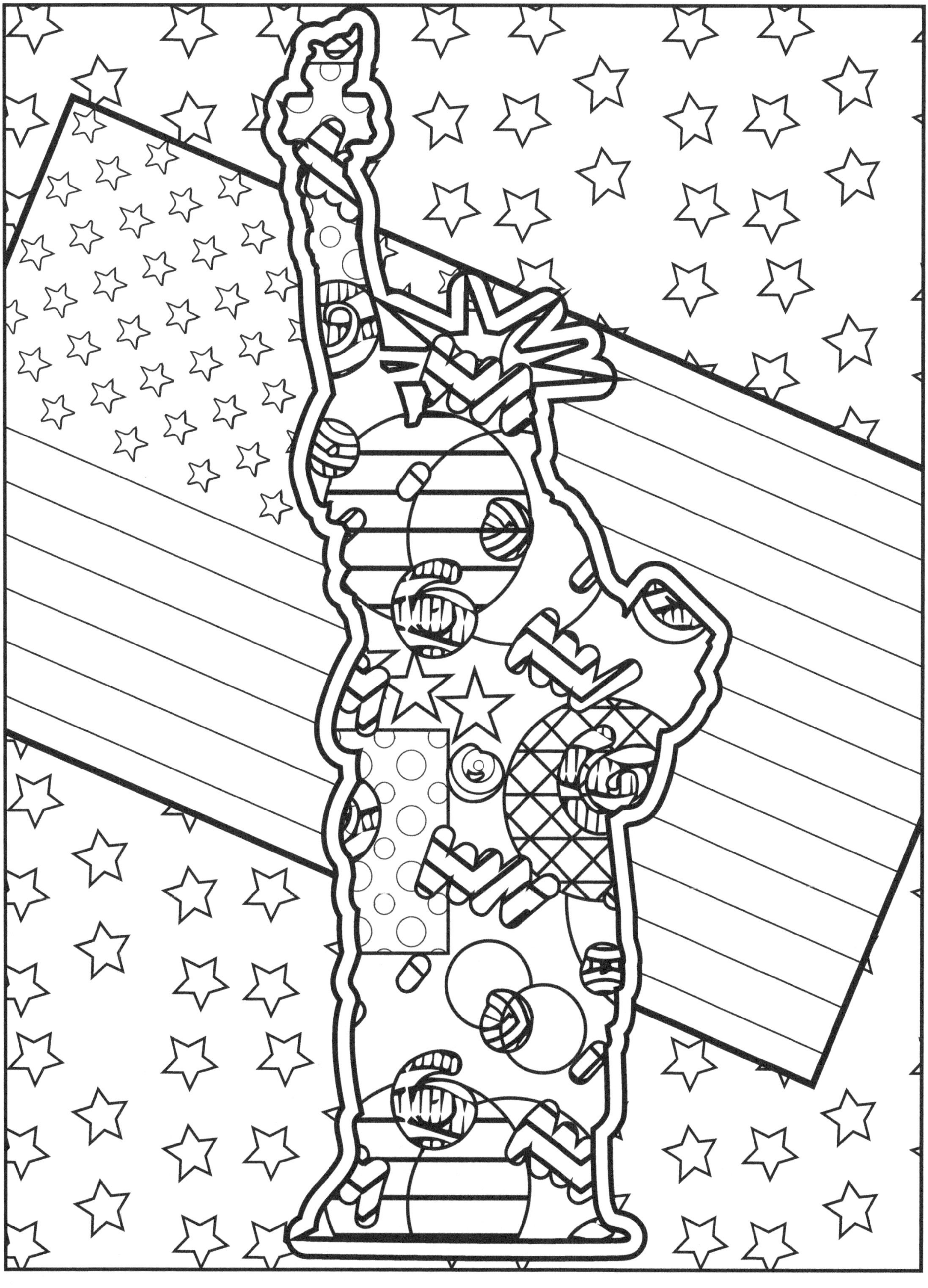

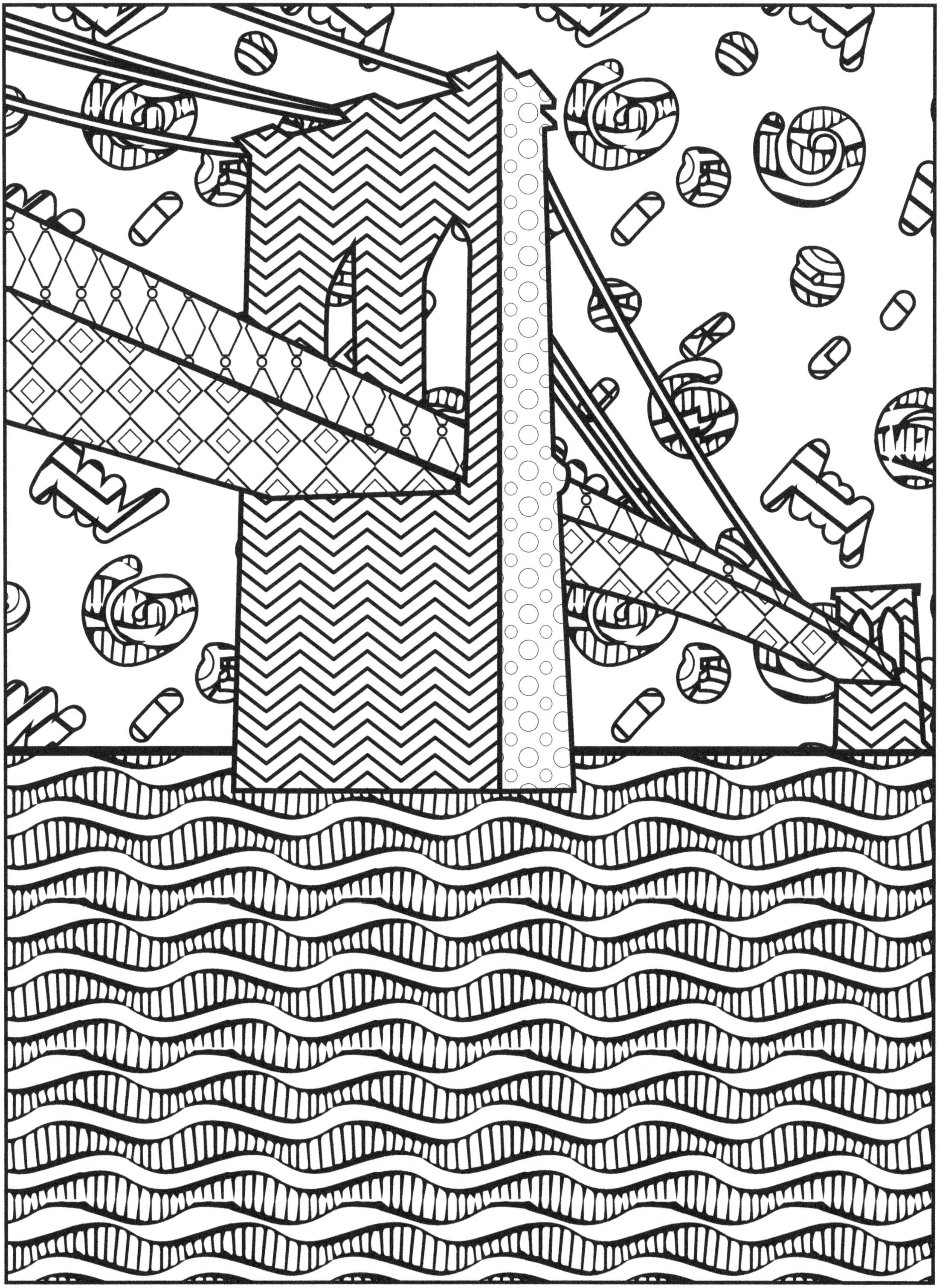

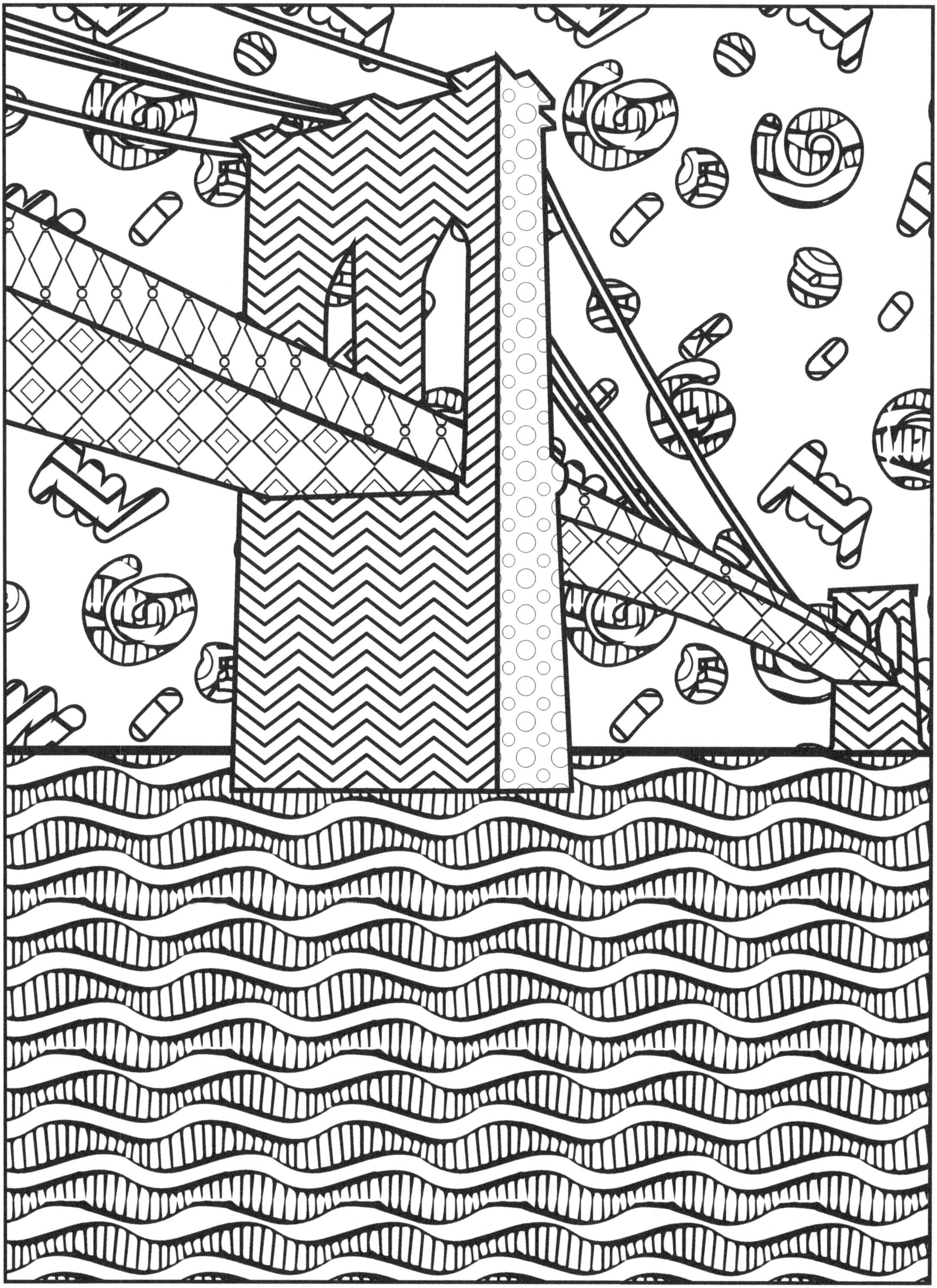

I ♥ NY

I ♥ NY

THE BIG APPLE

THE BIG APPLE

one way

one way

WANDERLUST

WANDERLUST

WANDERLUST

WANDERLUST

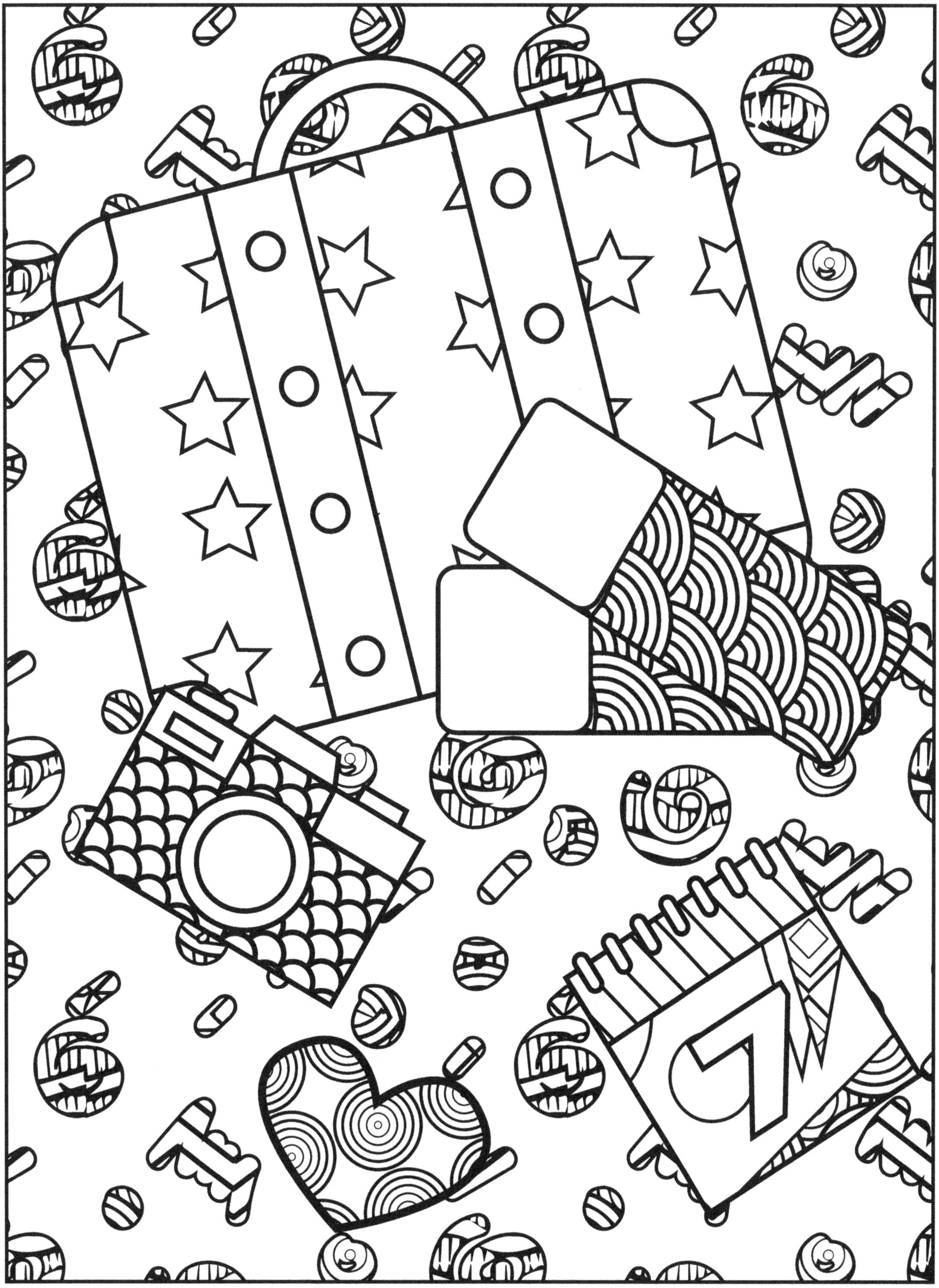

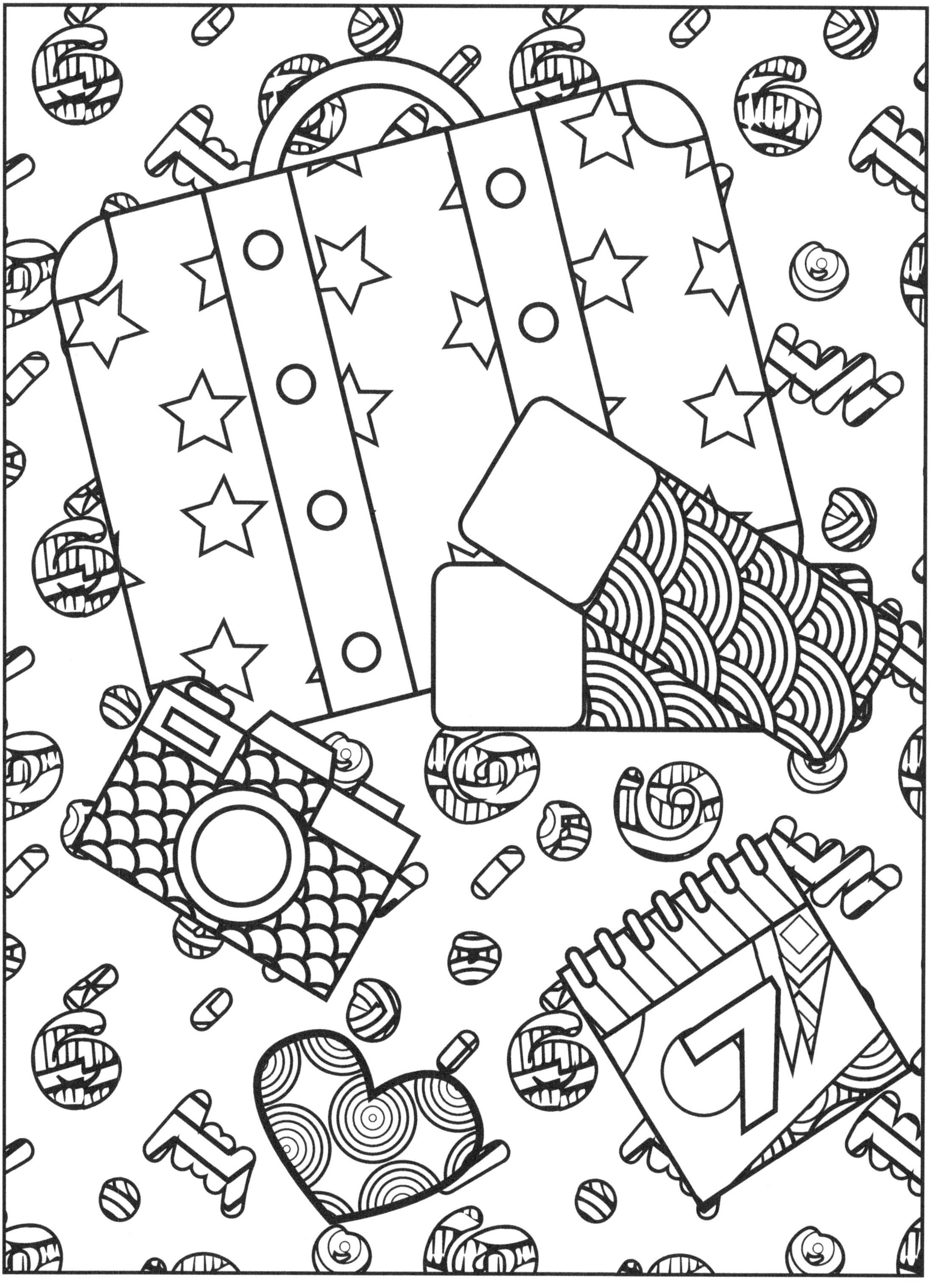

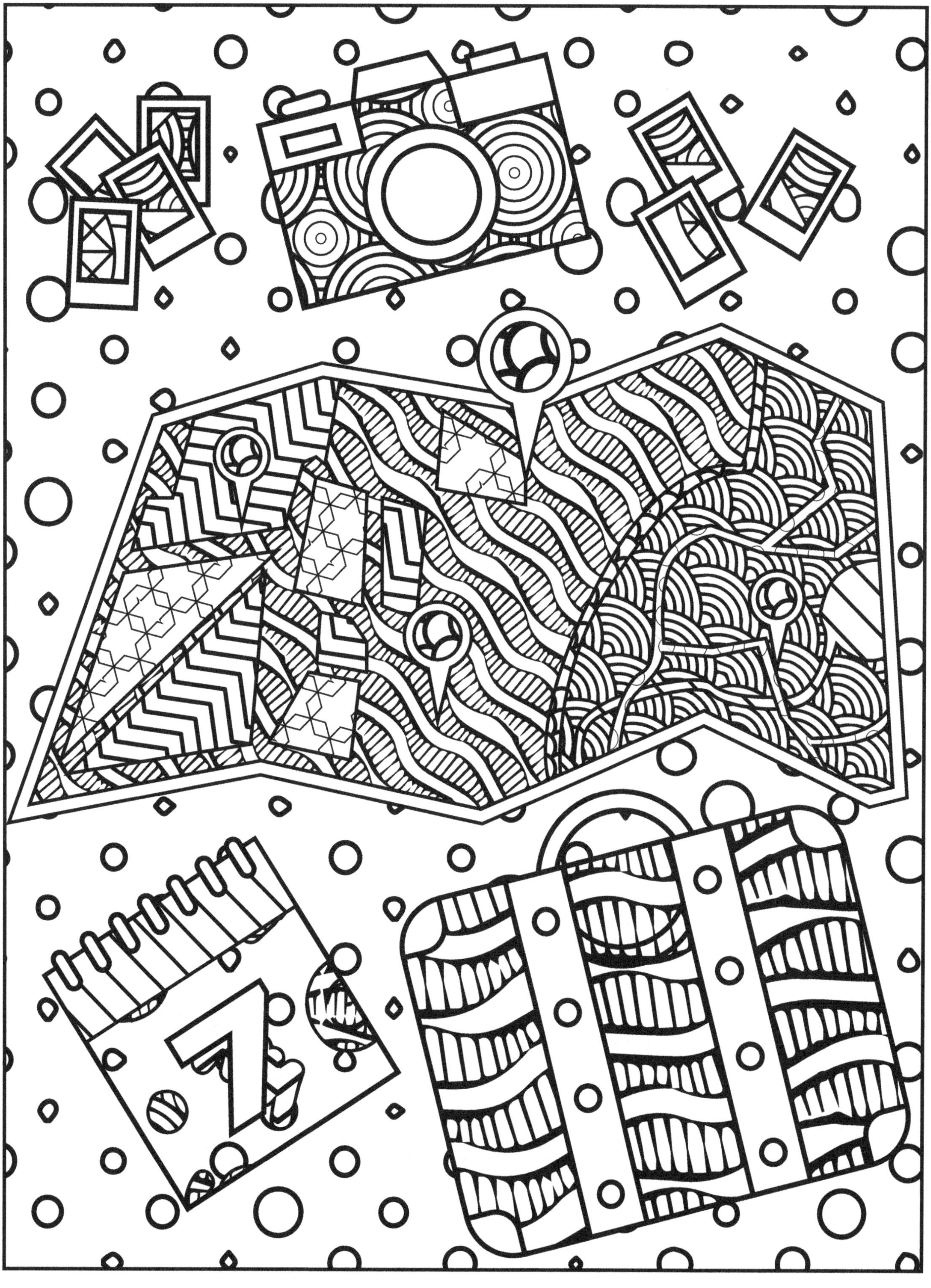

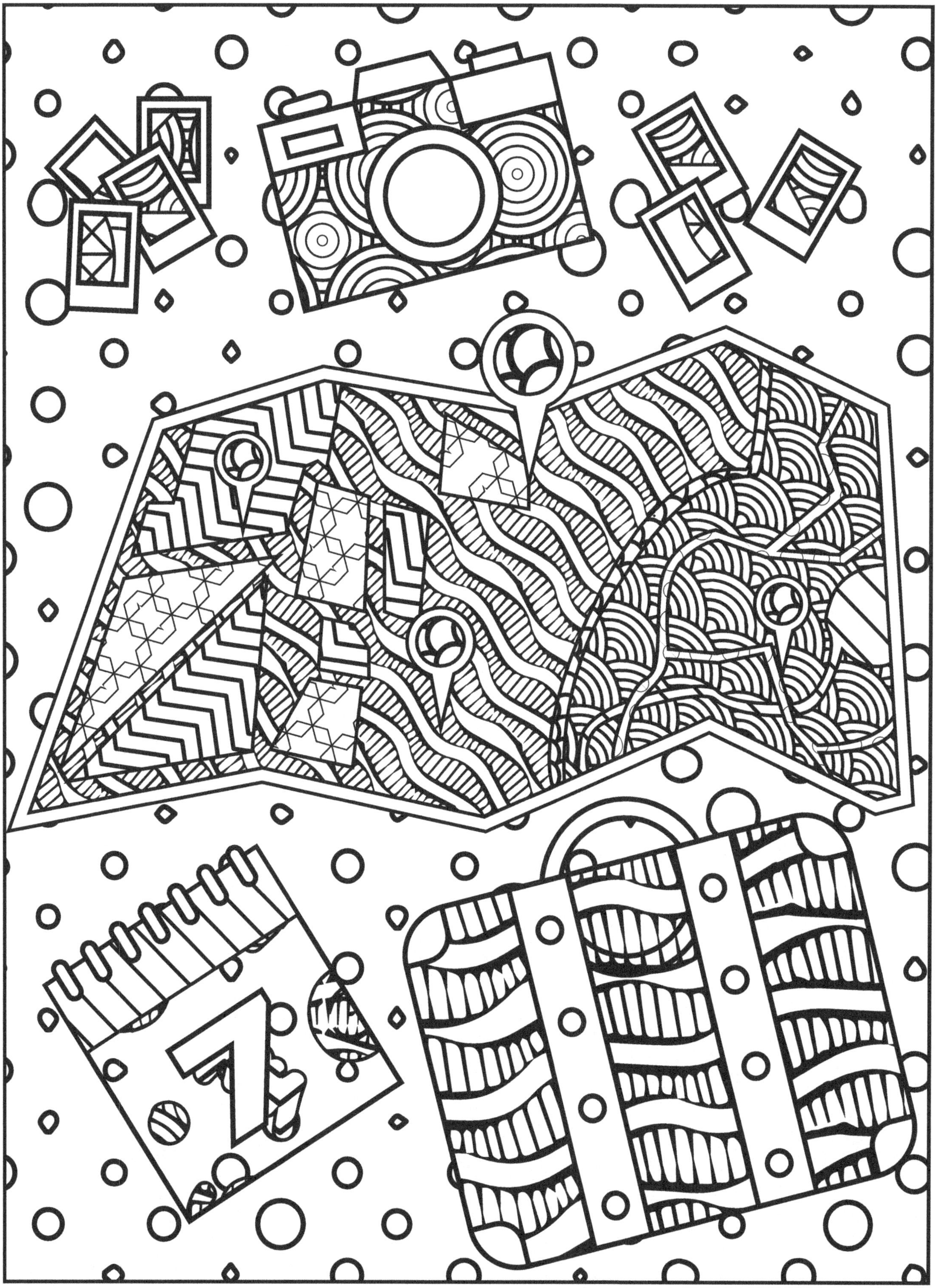
7

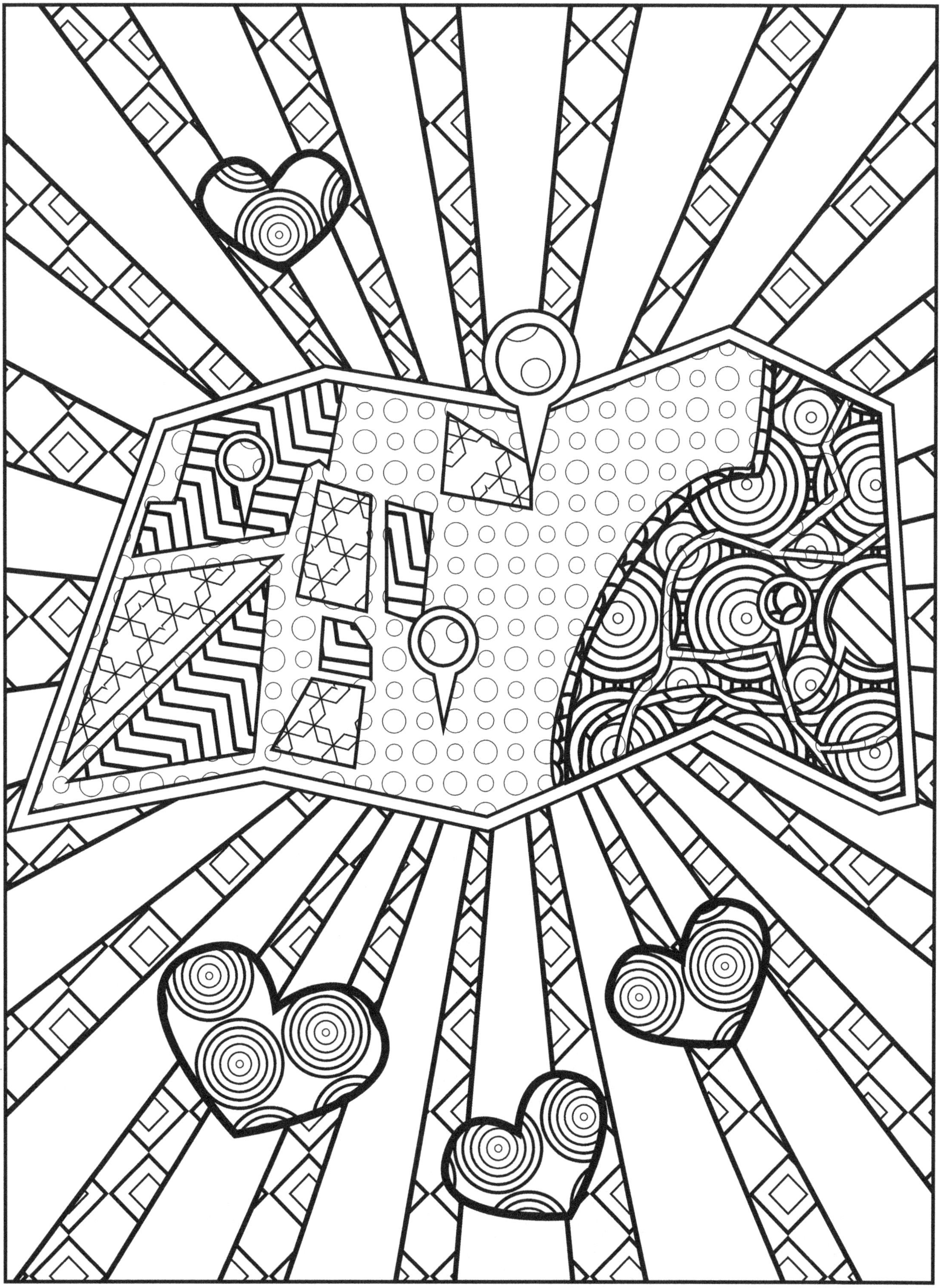

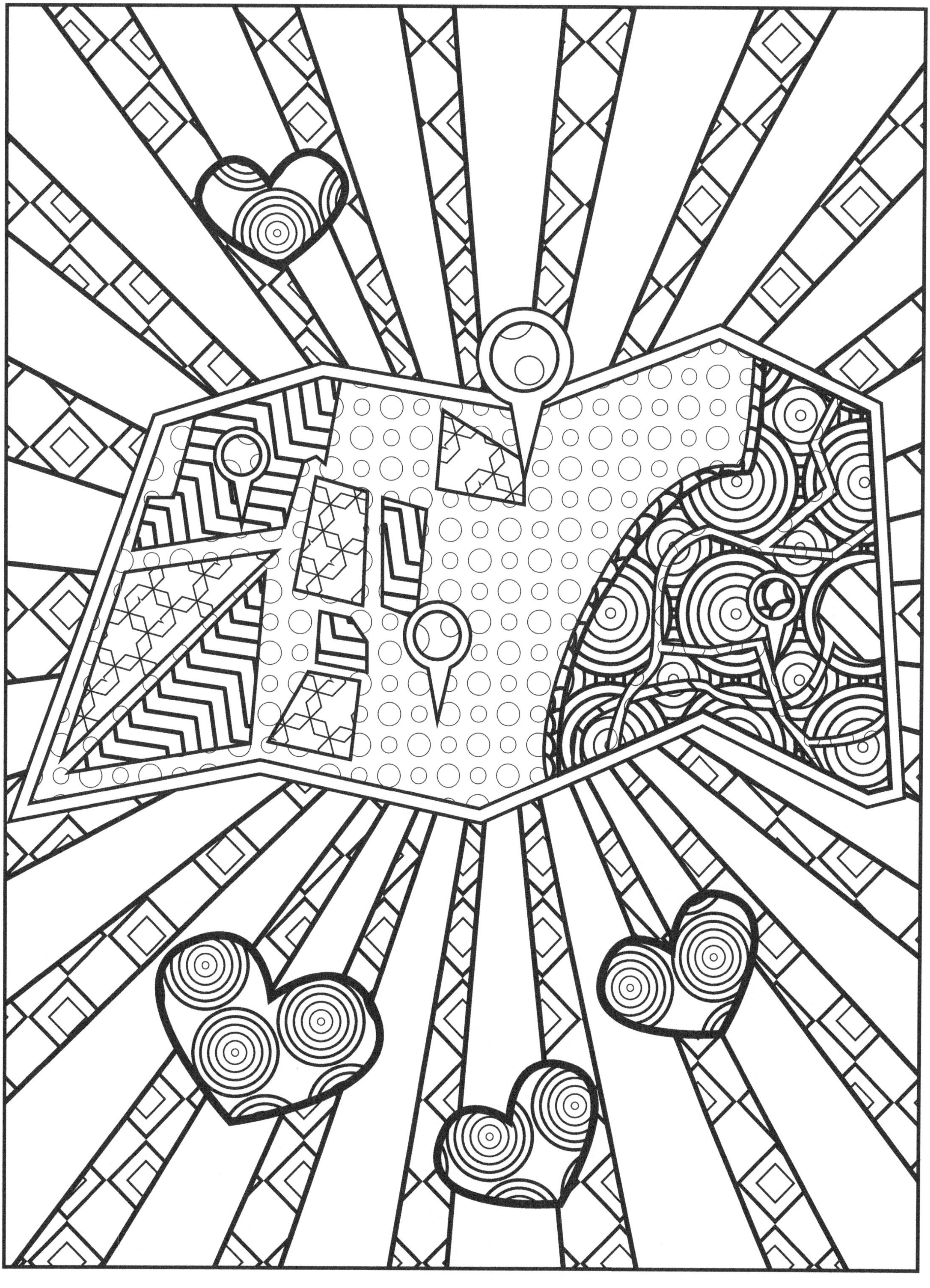

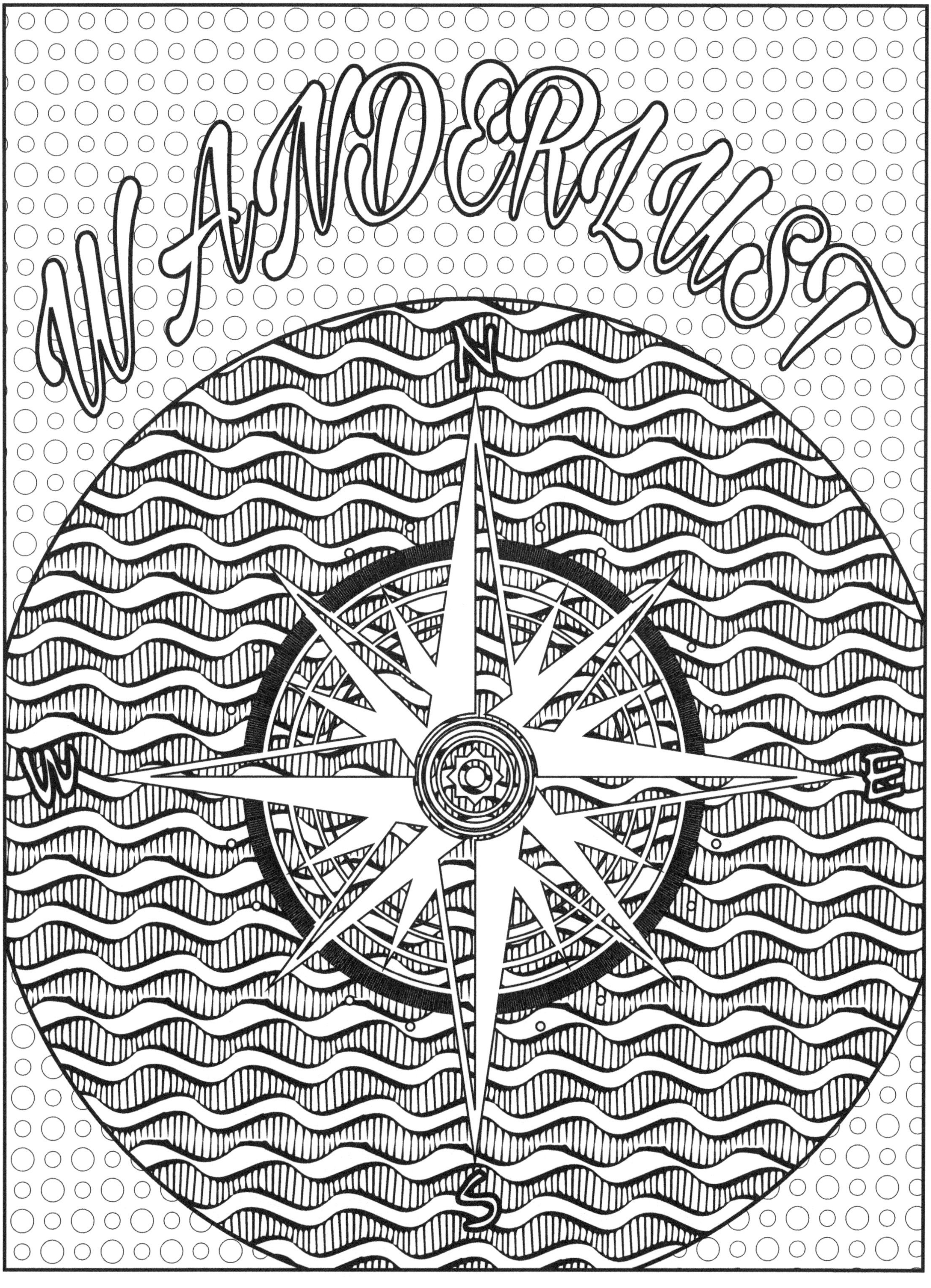
WANDERLUST
N
W
E
S

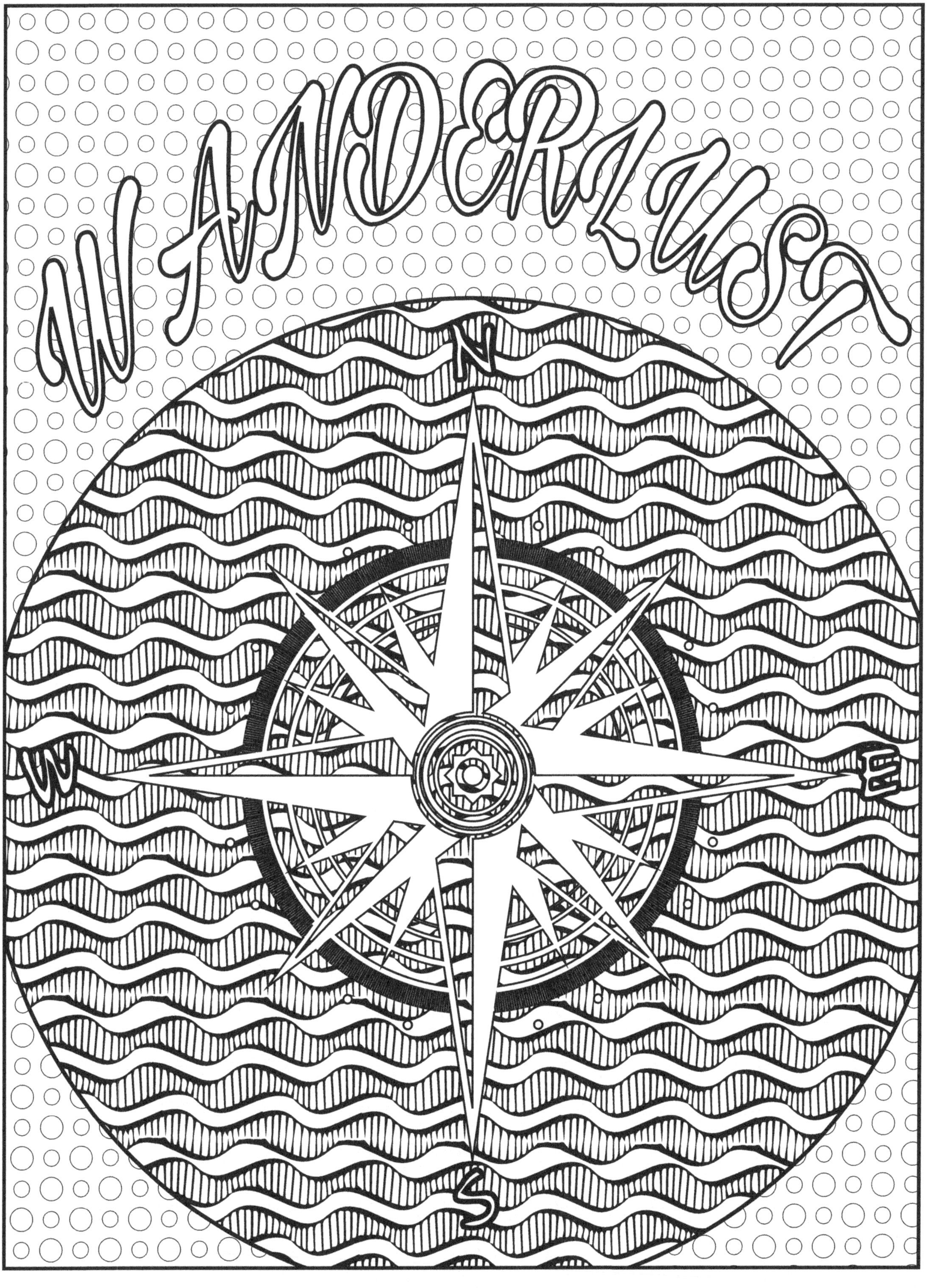
WANDERLUST
N
W
E
S

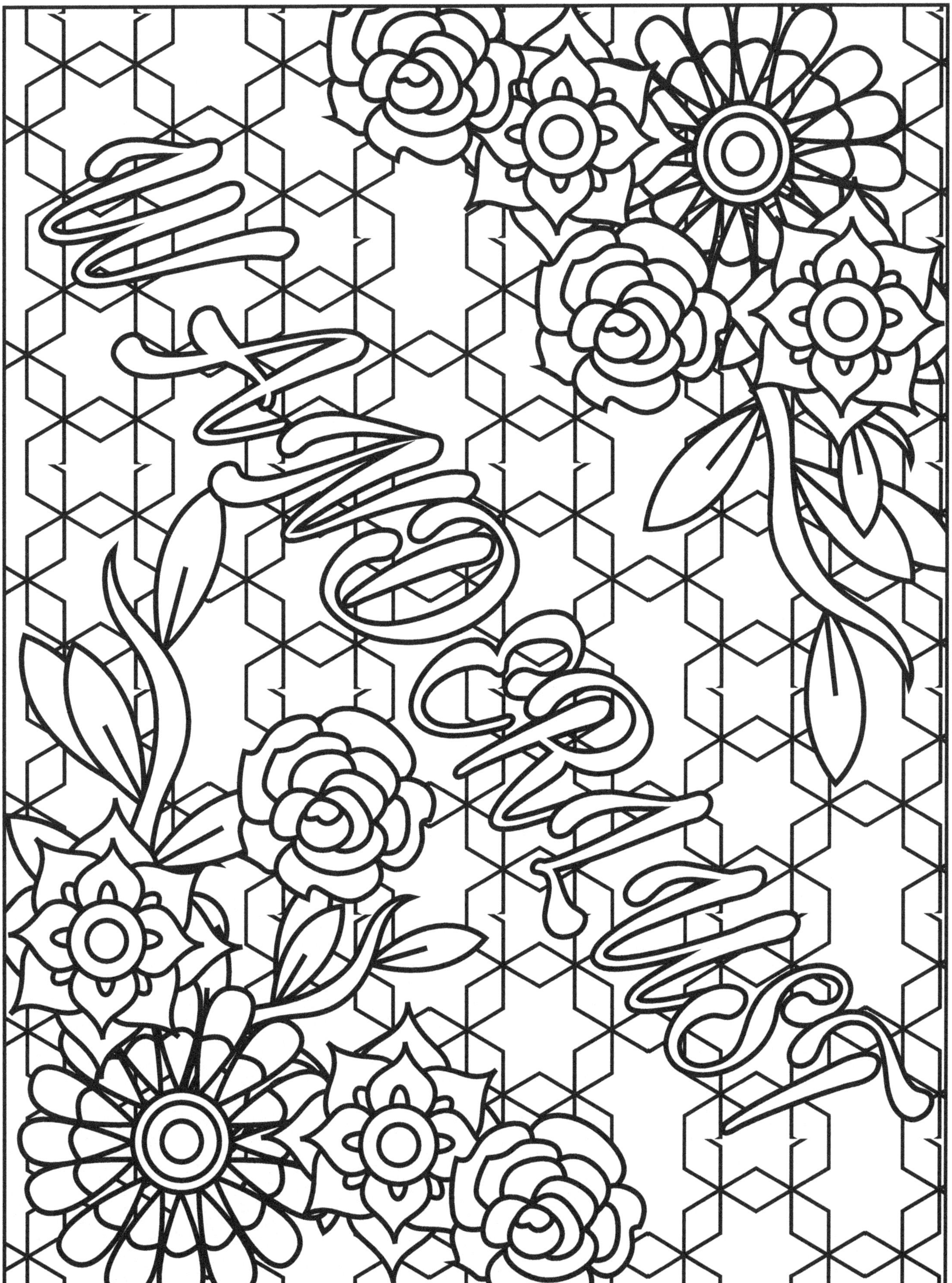

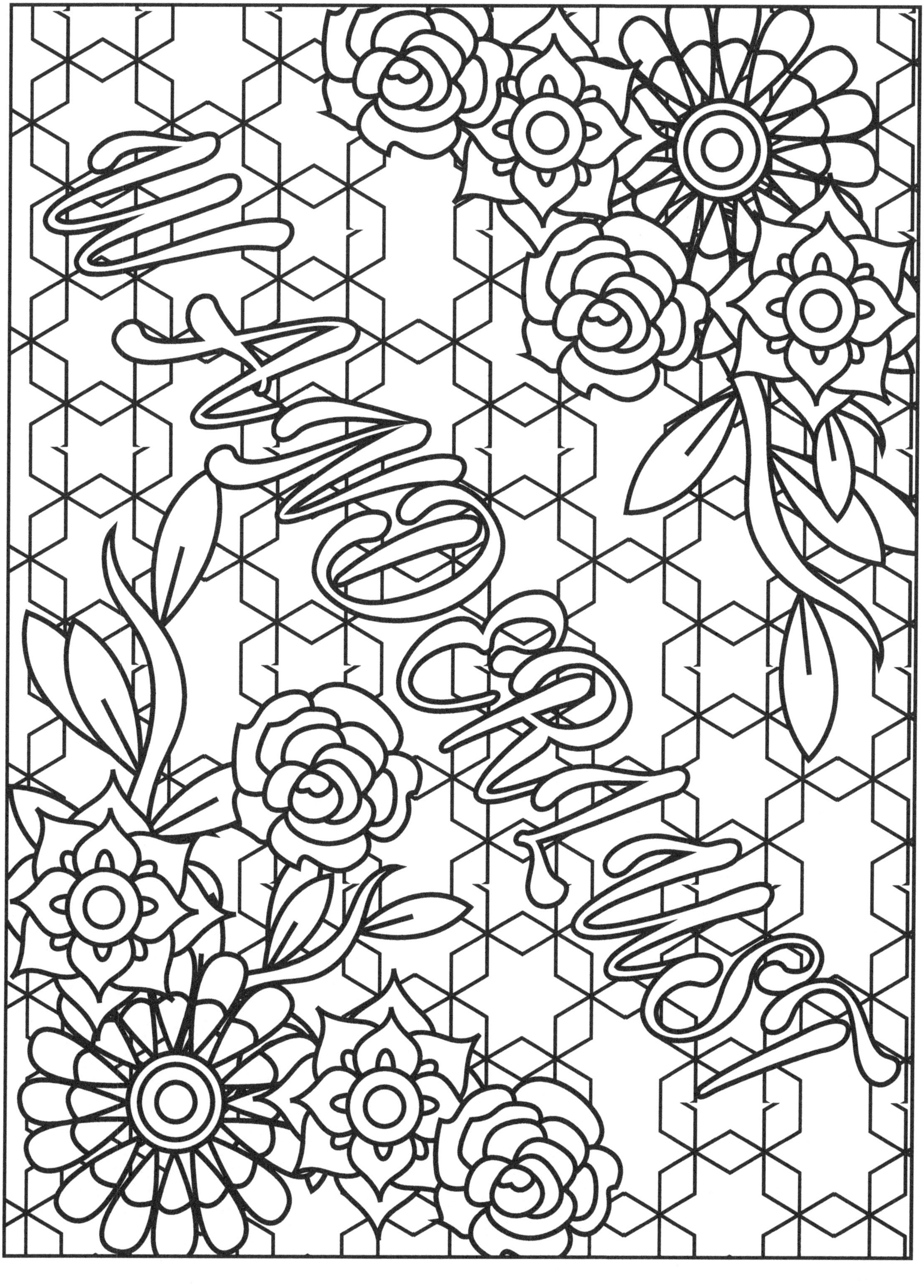

WANDERLUST

WANDERLUST

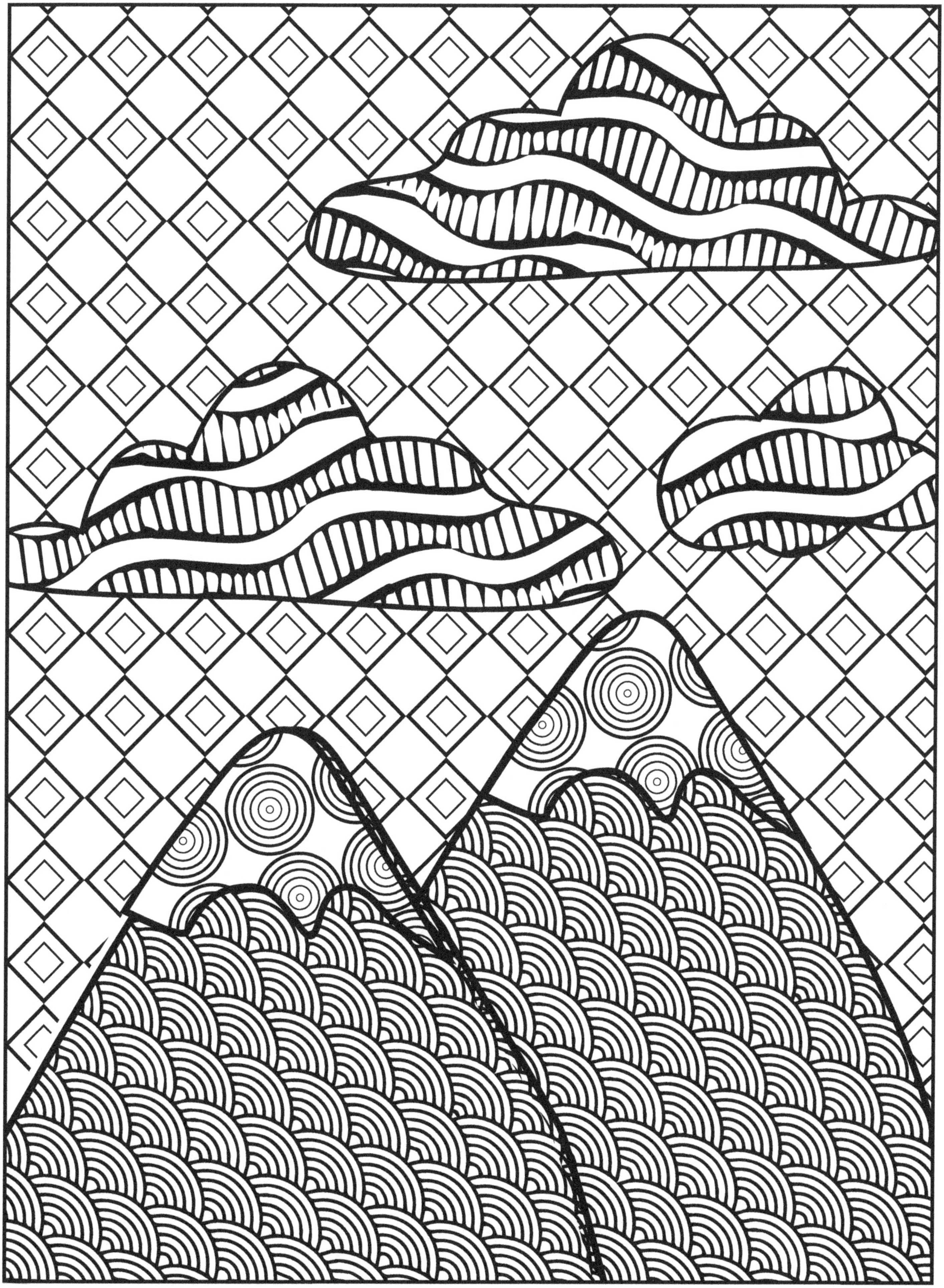

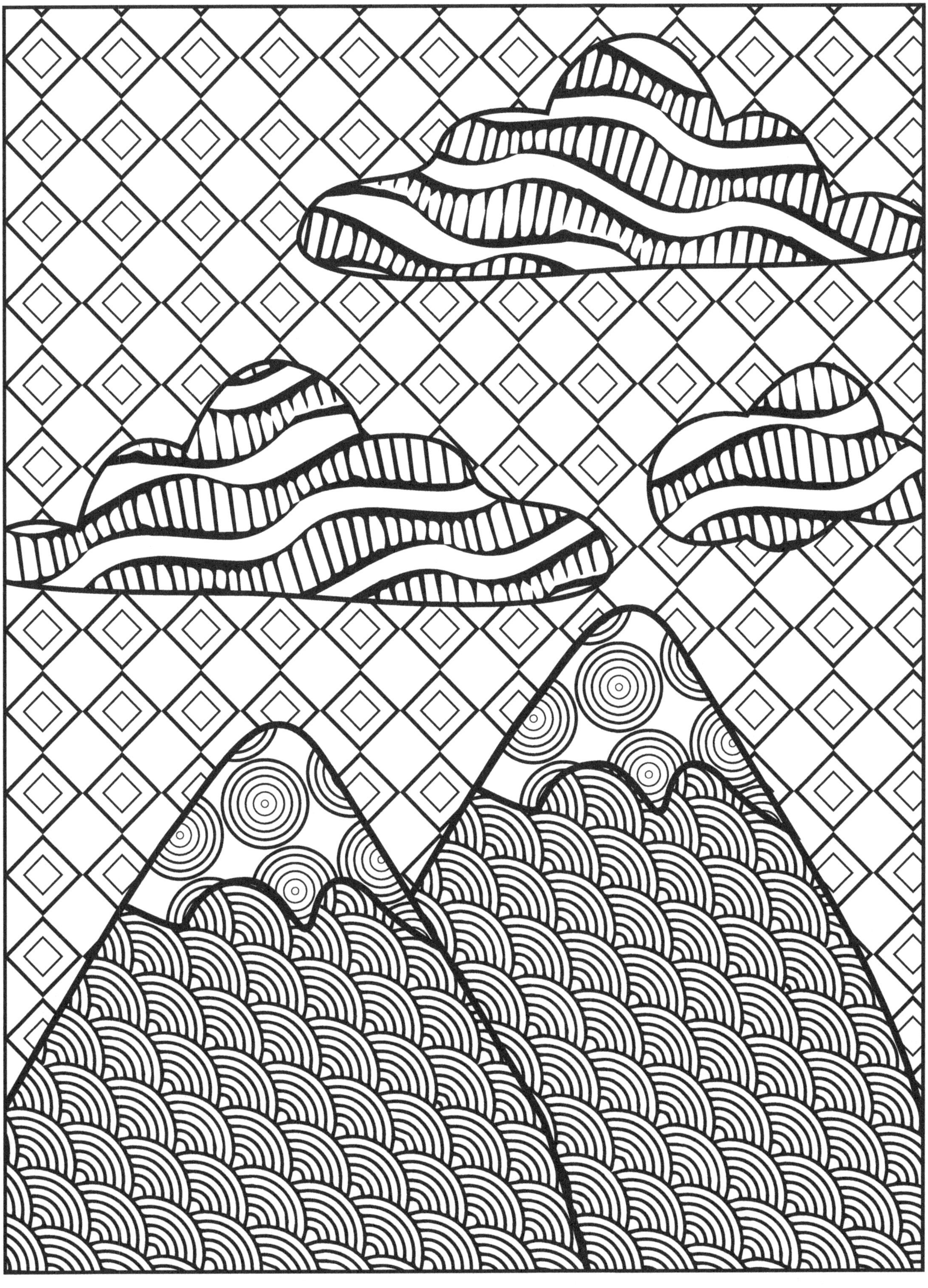

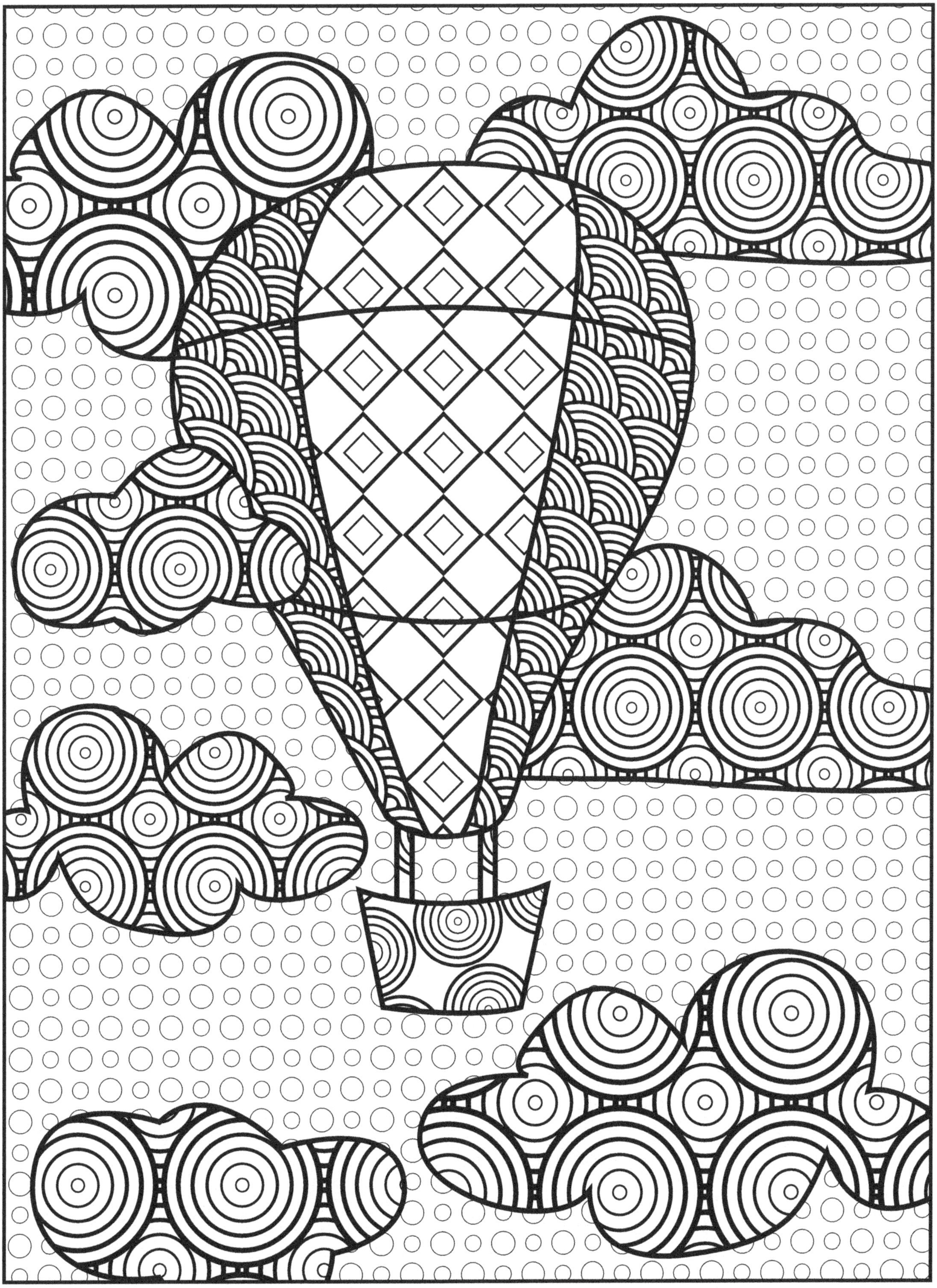

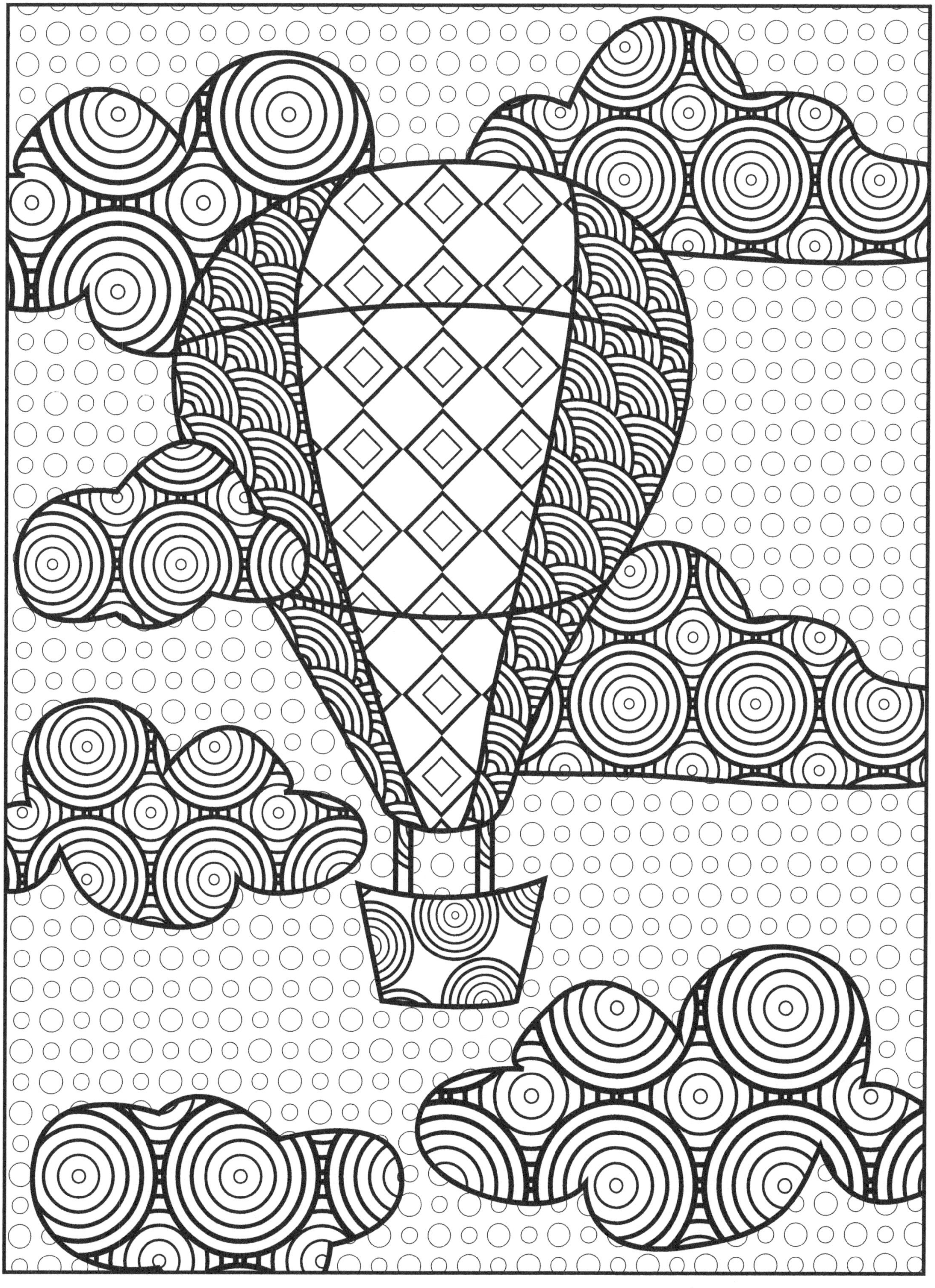

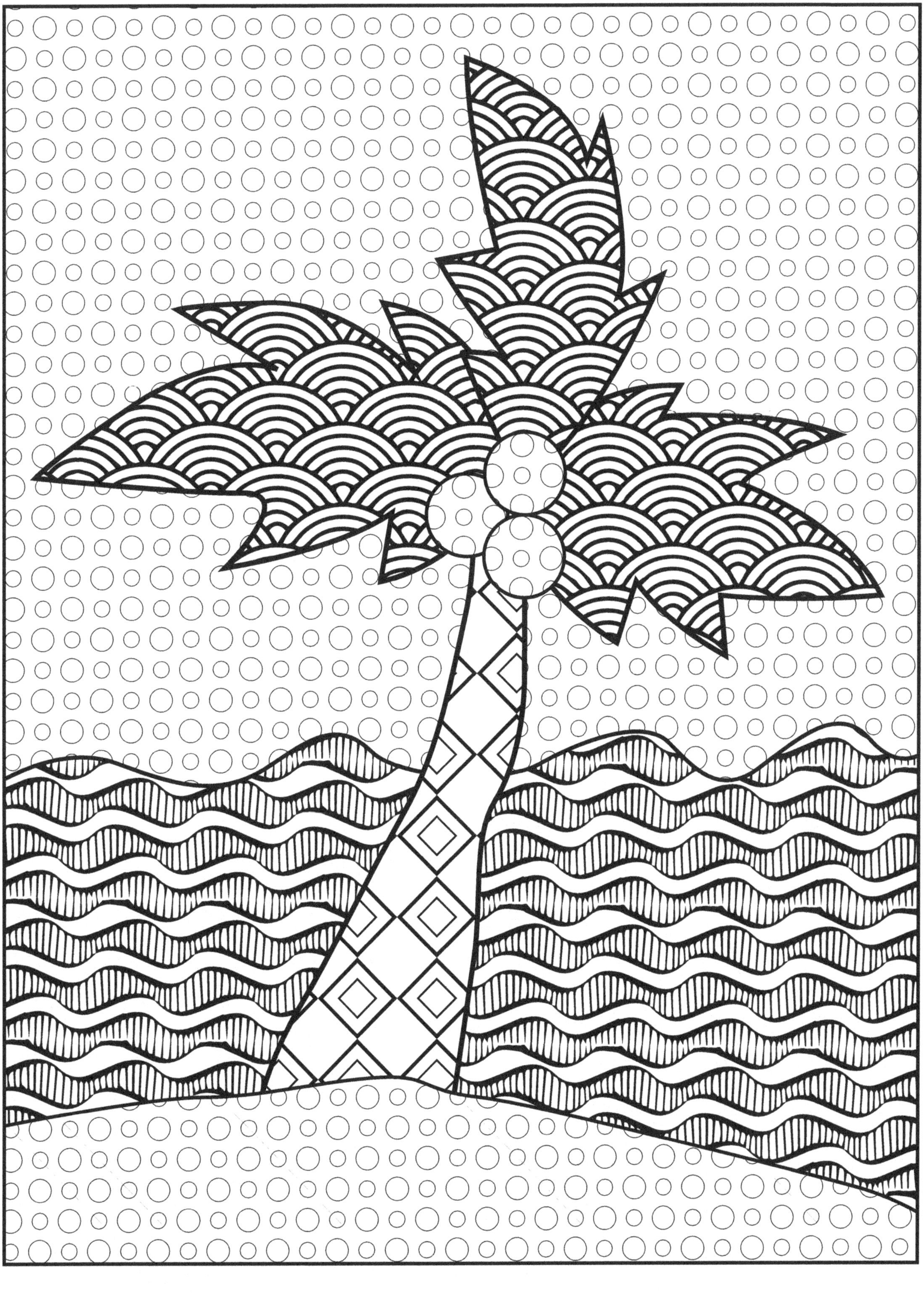

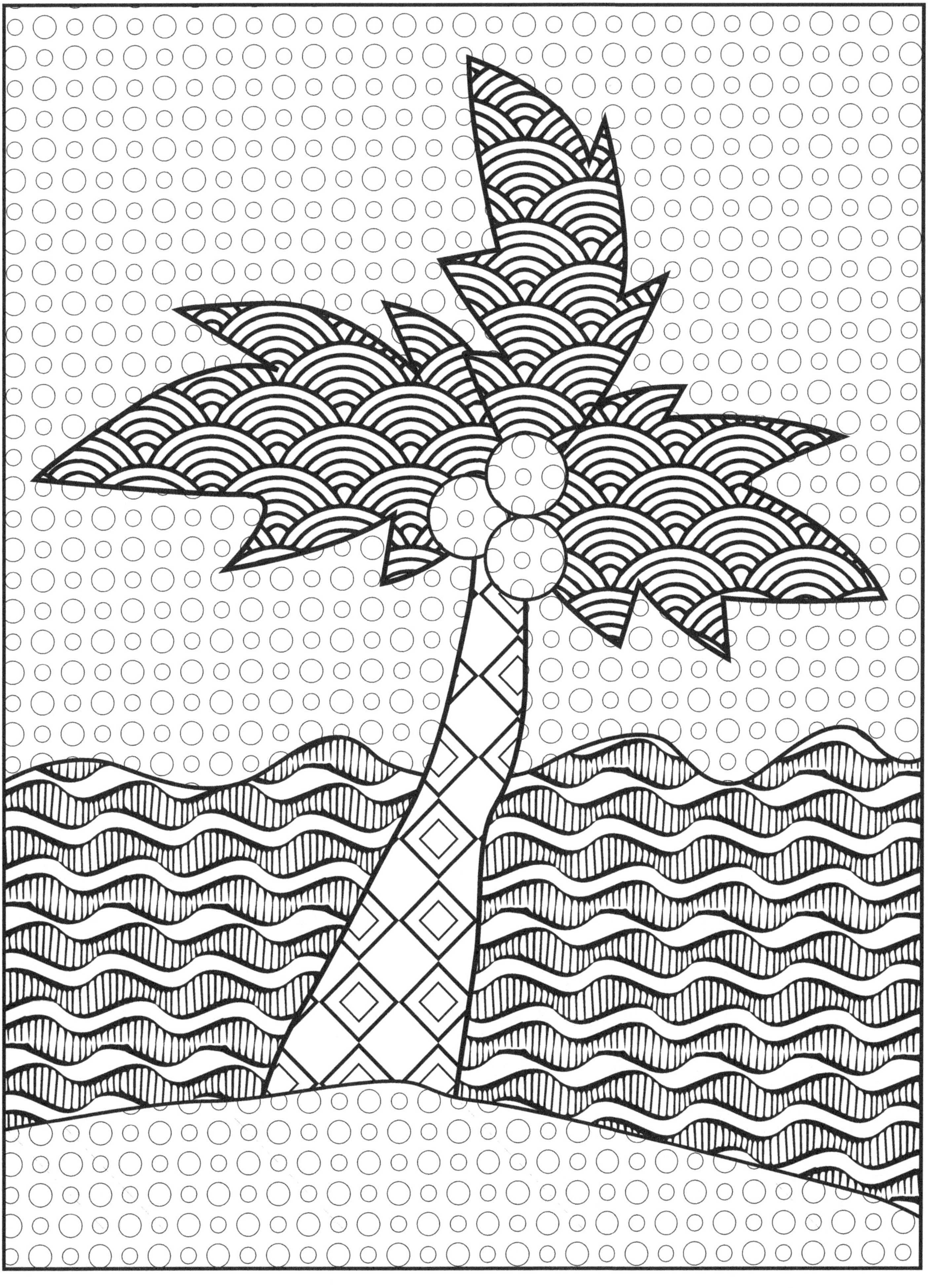

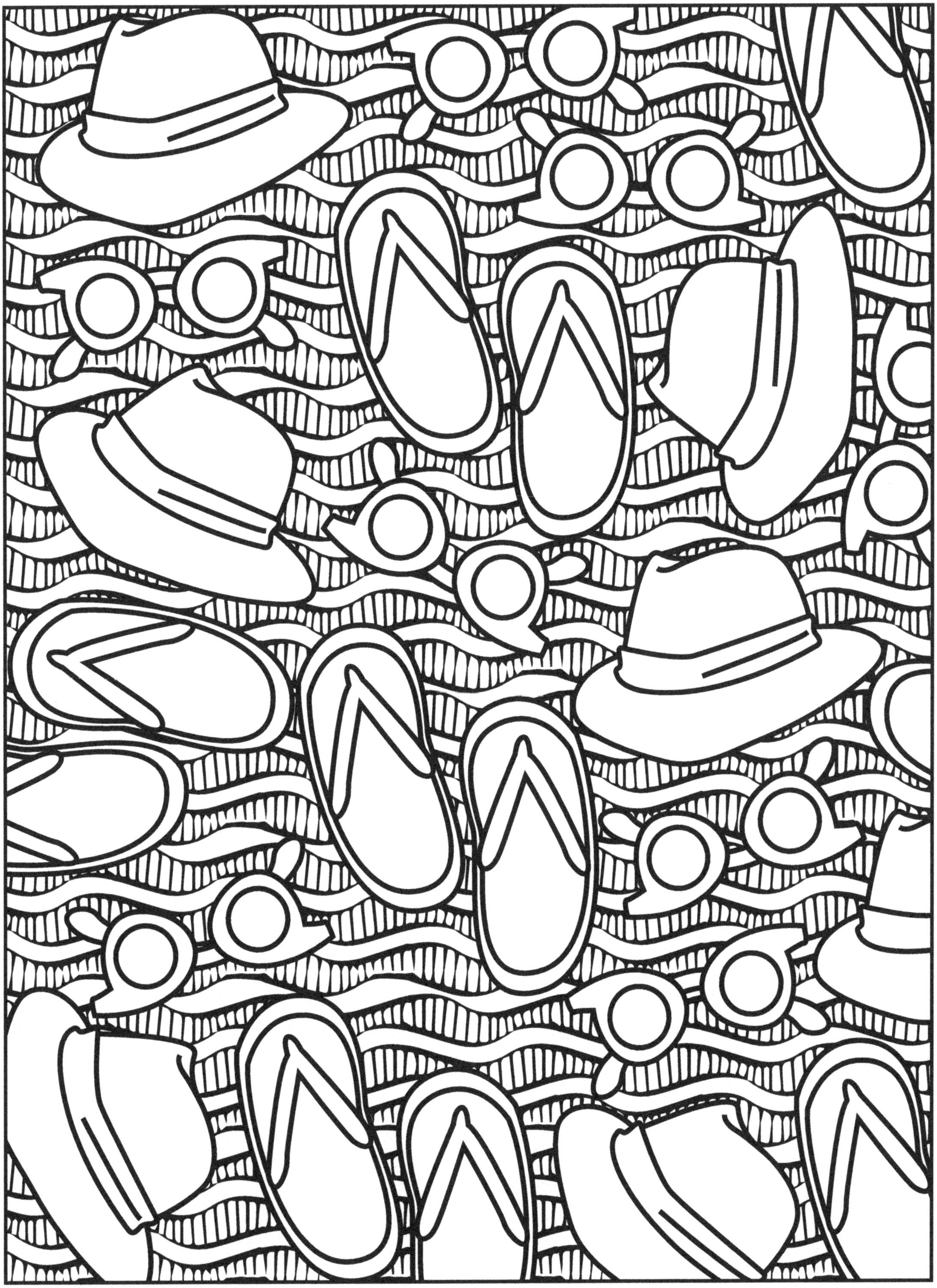

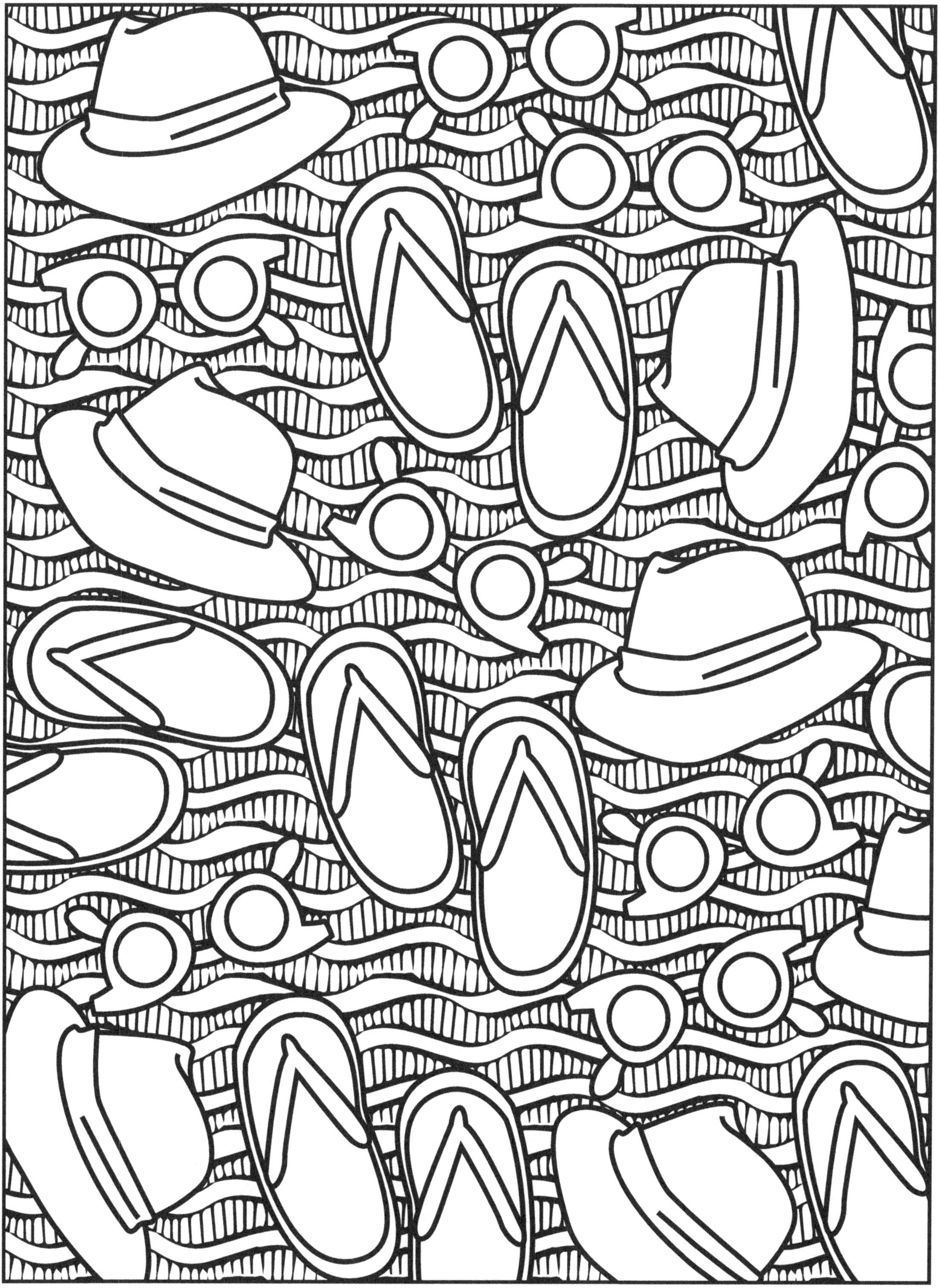

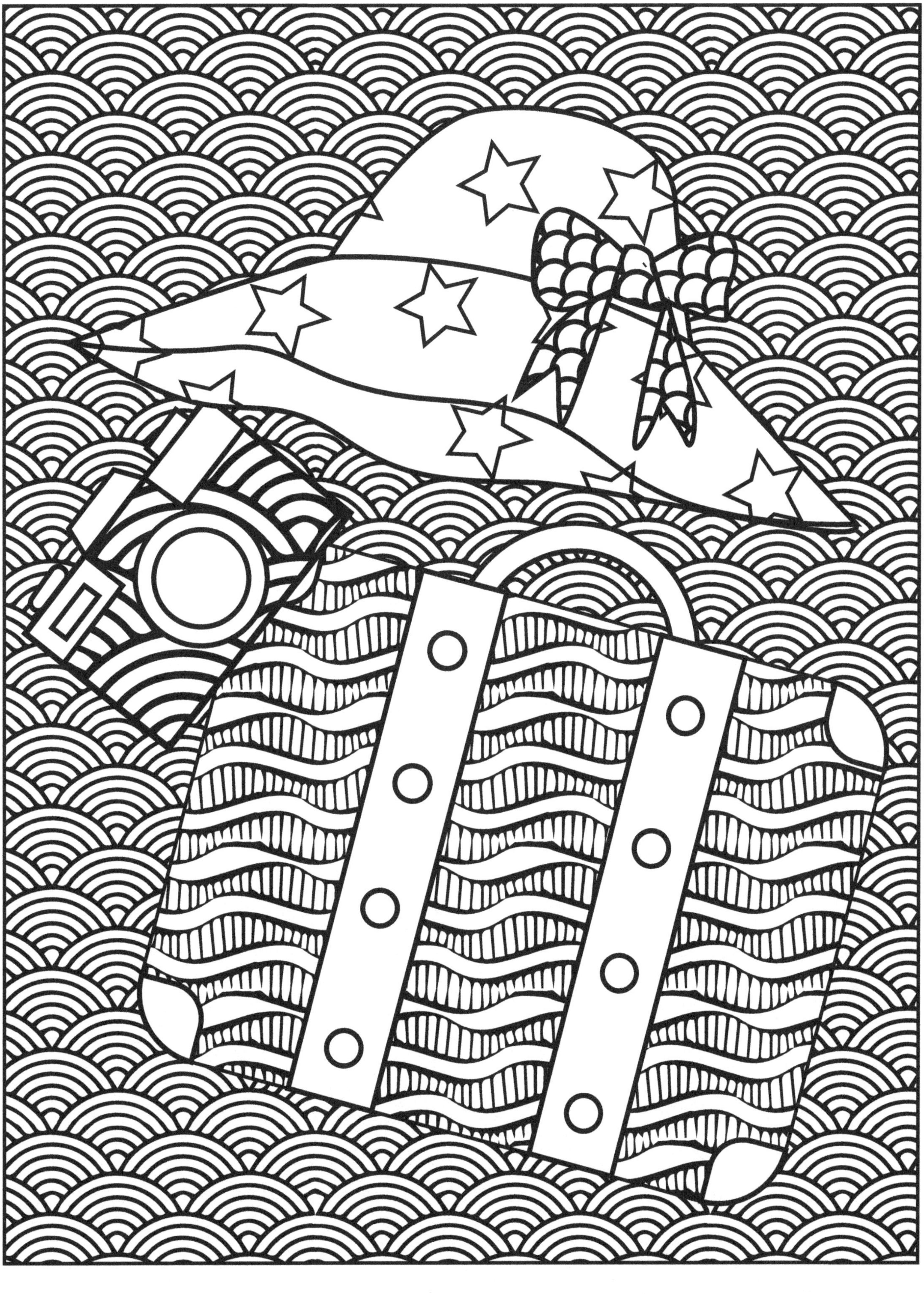

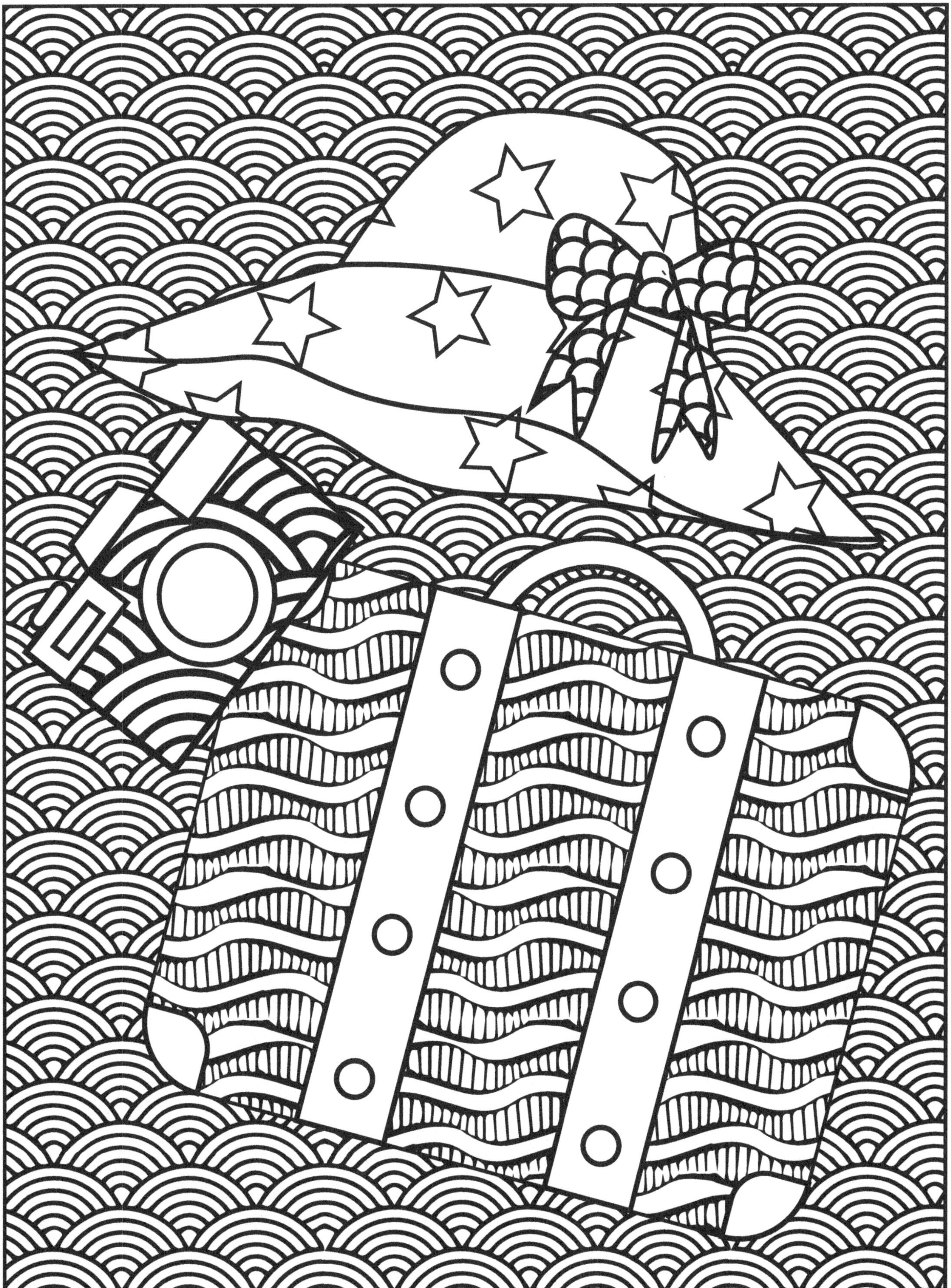

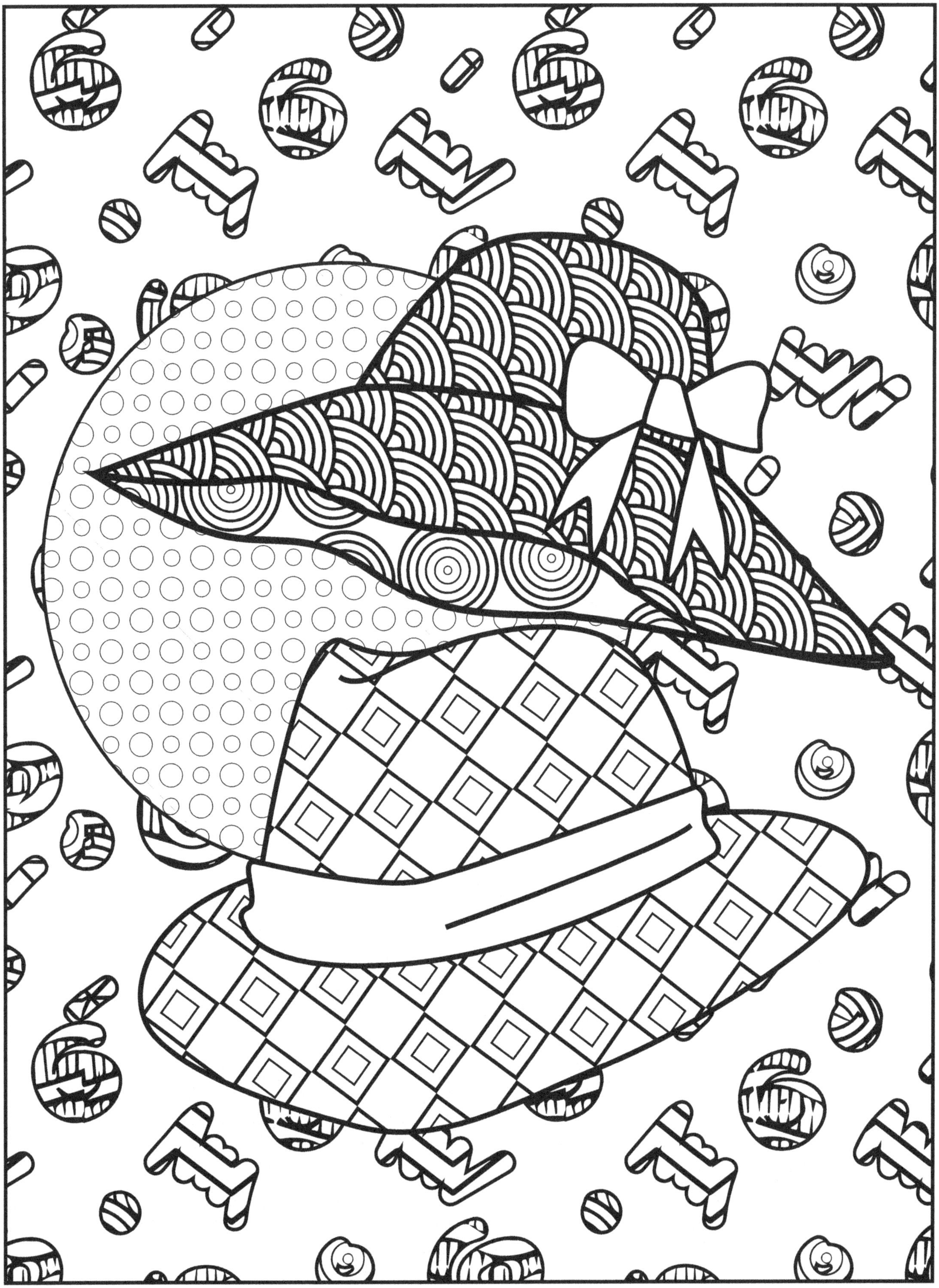

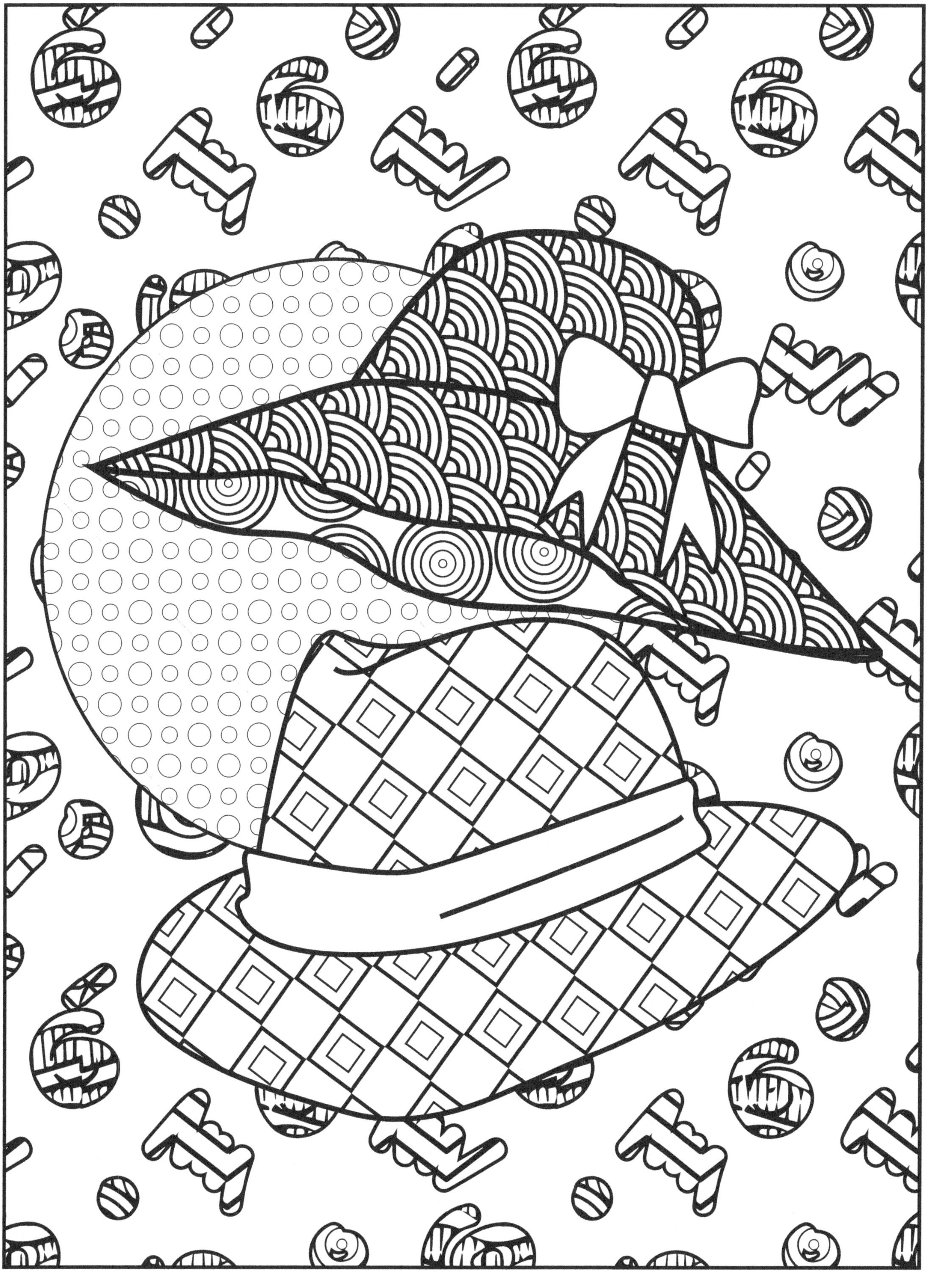

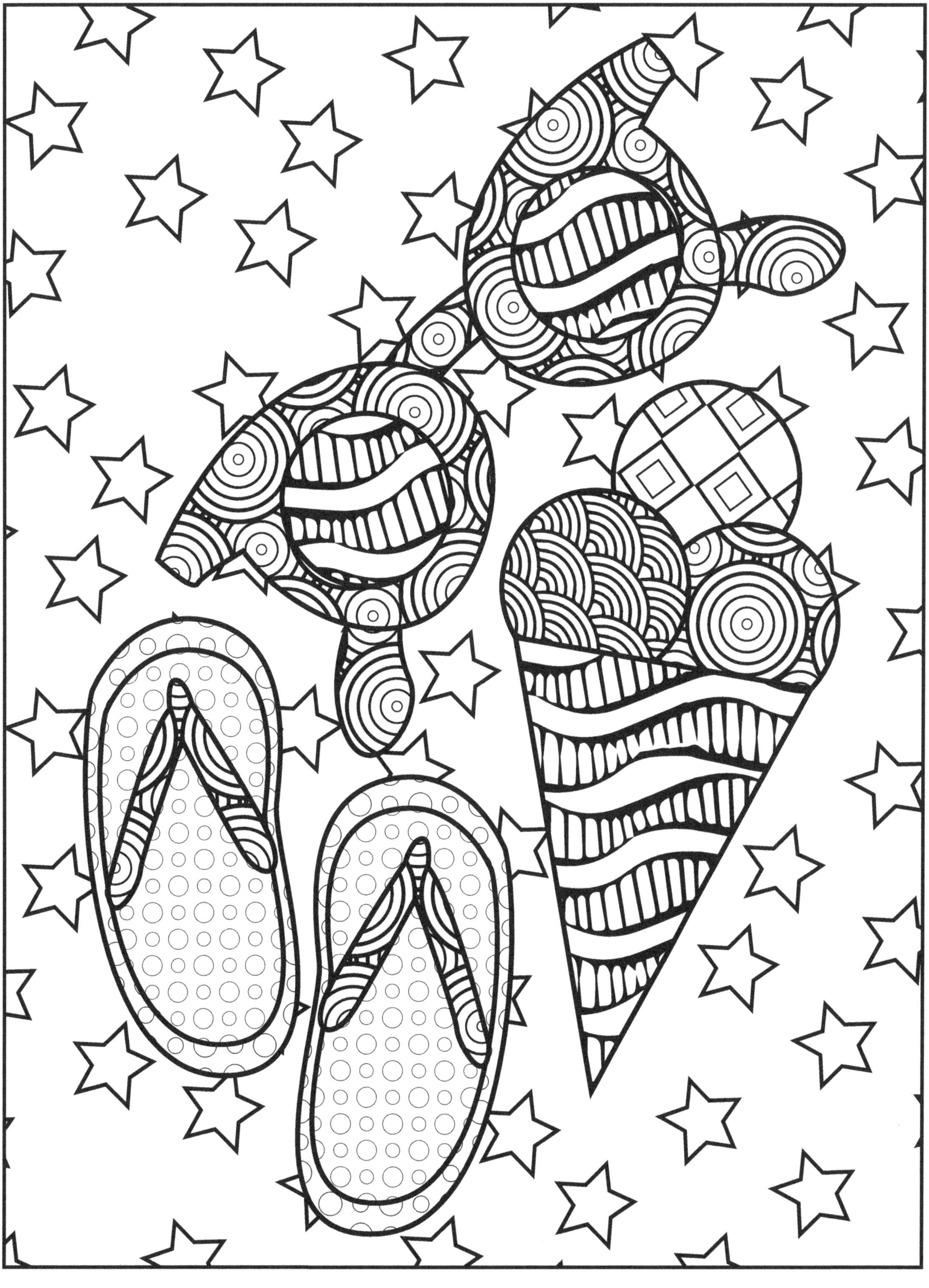

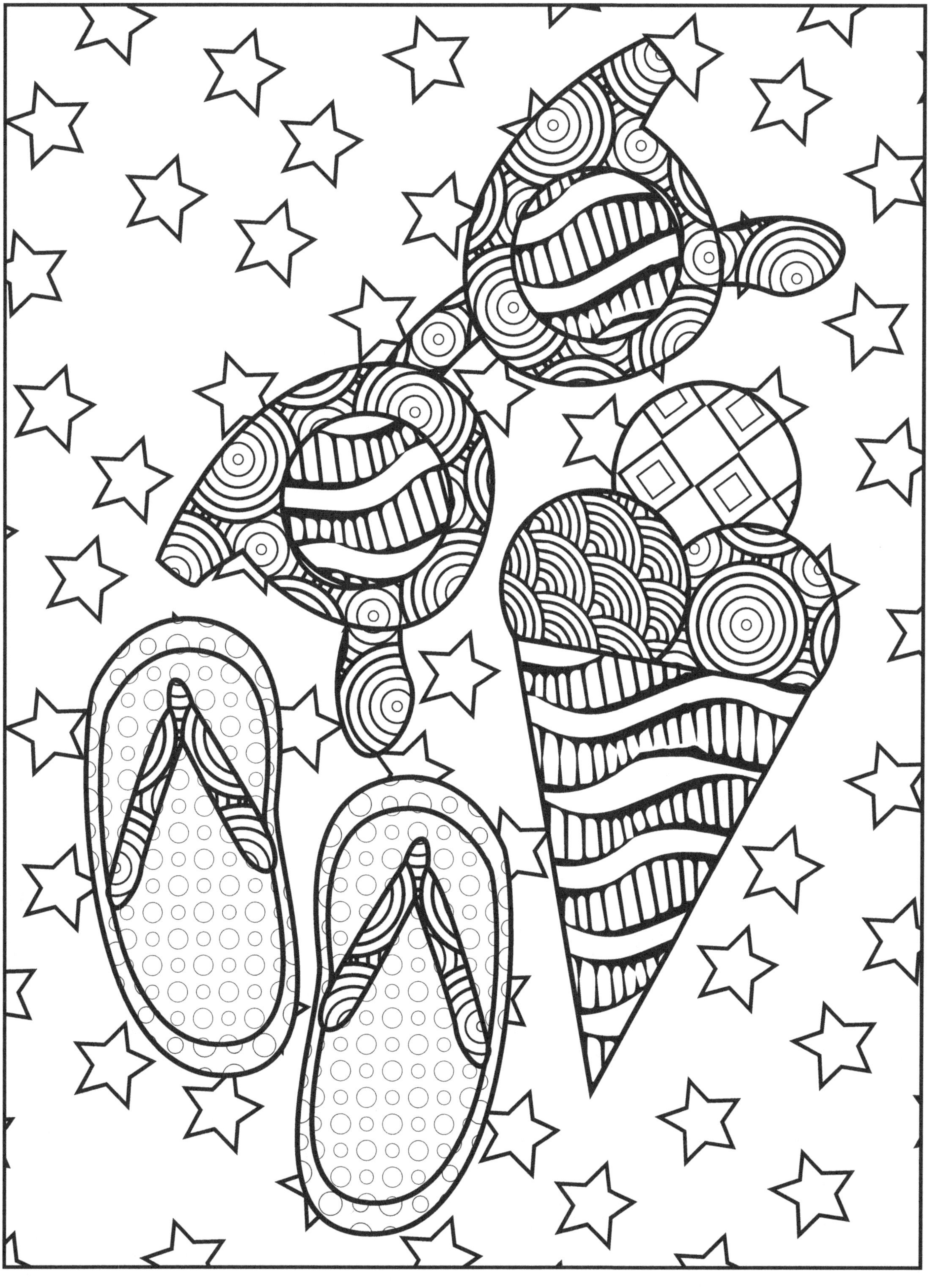

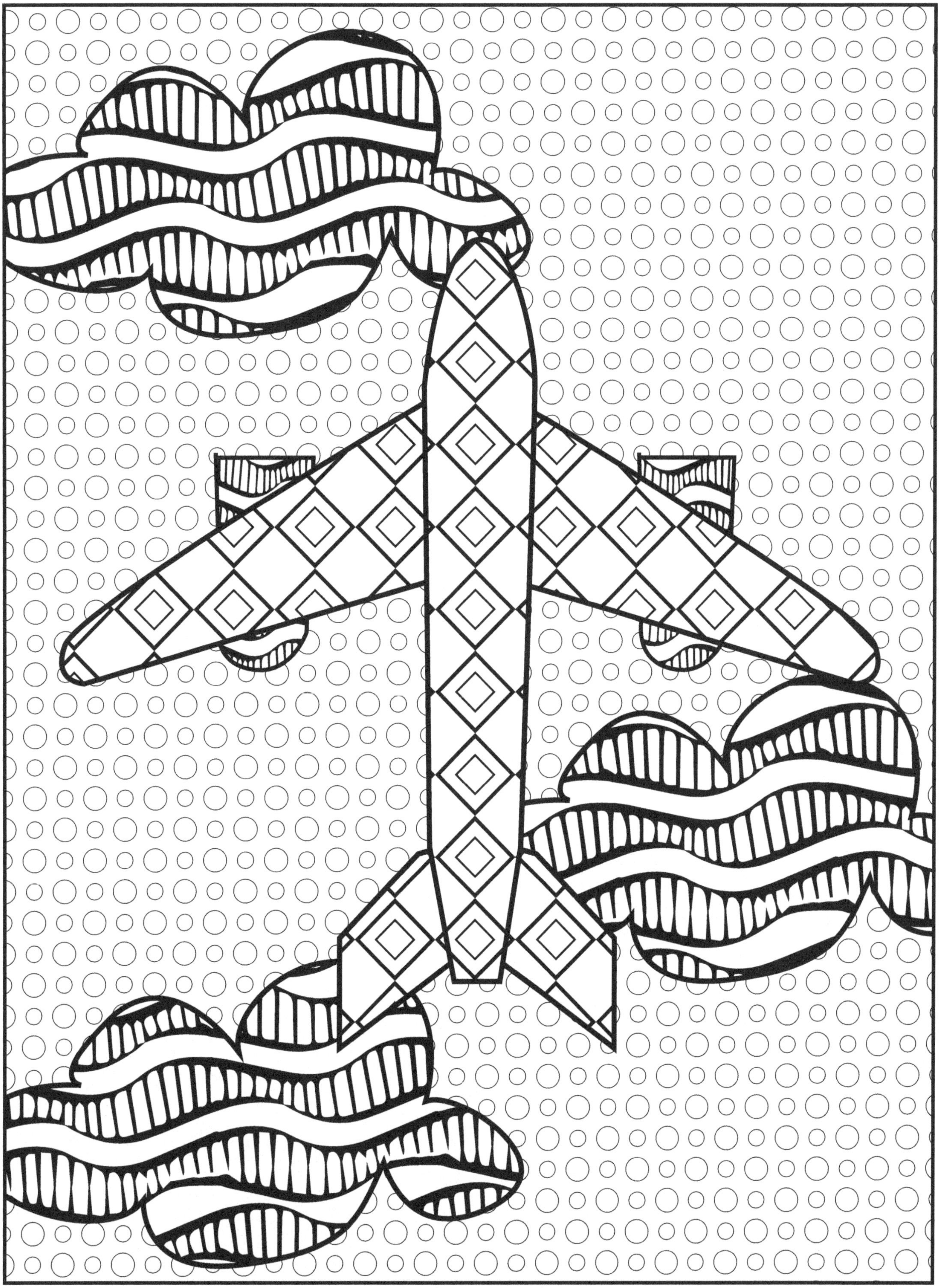

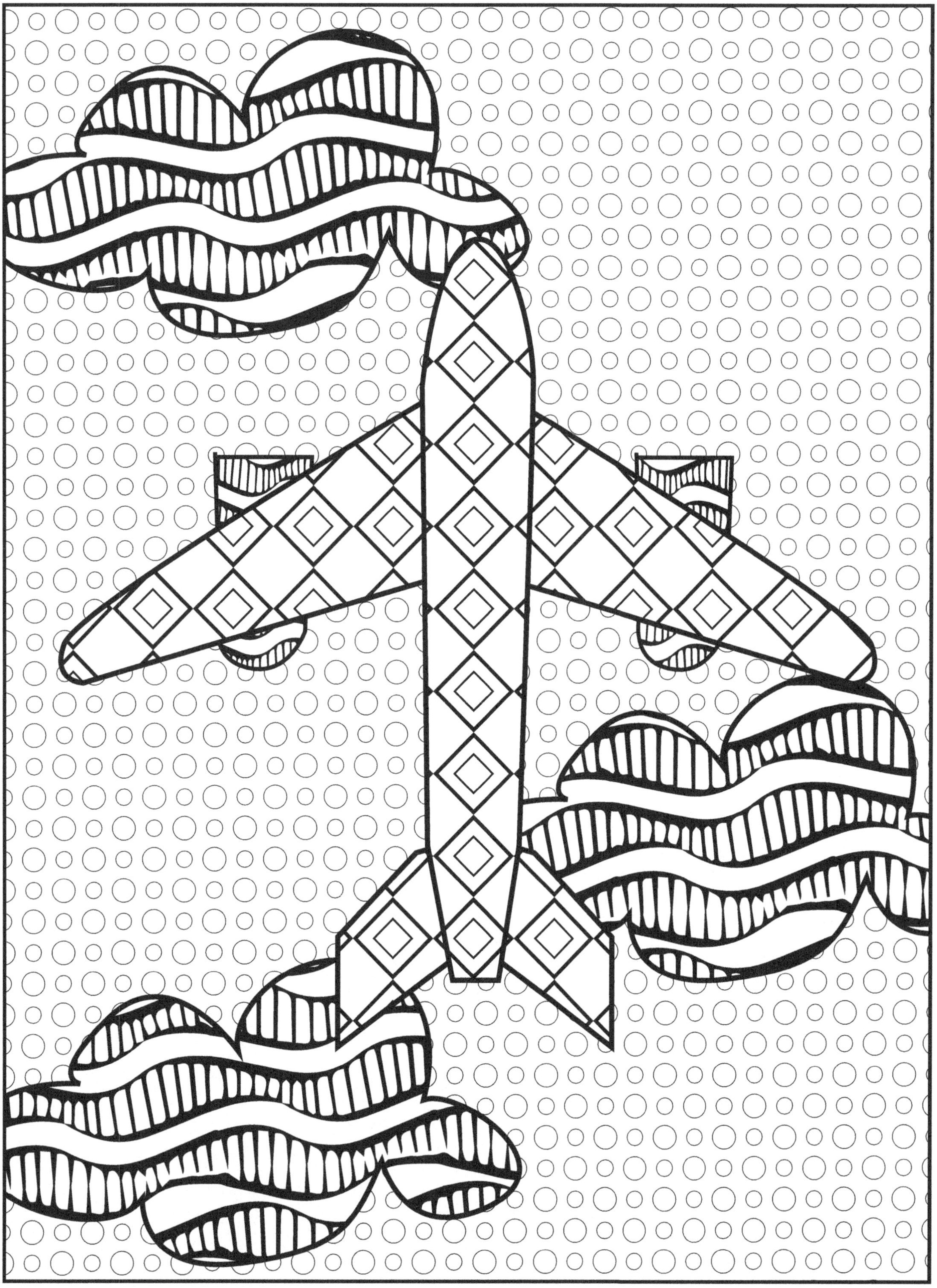

Made in United States
North Haven, CT
06 November 2021